insight text guide

Anica Boulanger-Mashberg

Requiem for a Beast

Matt Ottley

Copyright © Insight Publications 2022

First published in 2022.

Insight Publications Pty Ltd
3/350 Charman Road
Cheltenham VIC 3192
Australia
Tel: +61 3 8571 4950
Fax: +61 3 8571 0257
Email: books@insightpublications.com.au

www.insightpublications.com.au

Copying for educational purposes
The Australian *Copyright Act 1968* (the Act) allows a maximum of one chapter or 10% of this book, whichever is the greater, to be copied by any educational institution for its educational purposes provided that the educational institution (or the body that administers it) has given a remuneration notice to Copyright Agency under the Act.

For details of the Copyright Agency licence for educational institutions contact:

Copyright Agency
Tel: +61 2 9394 7600
Fax: +61 2 9394 7601
www.copyright.com.au

Copying for other purposes
Except as permitted under the Act (for example, any fair dealing for the purposes of study, research, criticism or review) no part of this book may be reproduced, stored in a retrieval system, or transmitted in any form or by any means without prior written permission. All inquiries should be made to the publisher at the address above.

A catalogue record for this book is available from the National Library of Australia

Matt Ottley's Requiem for a Beast / Anica Boulanger-Mashberg

Anica Boulanger-Mashberg asserts the moral right to be identified as the author of this work.

ISBNs:
9781922771230 (print)
9781922771247 (digital)
9781922771254 (bundle: print + digital)

Cover design by Melisa Paredes

Printed in Australia by Ligare Book Printers

contents

CHARACTER MAP

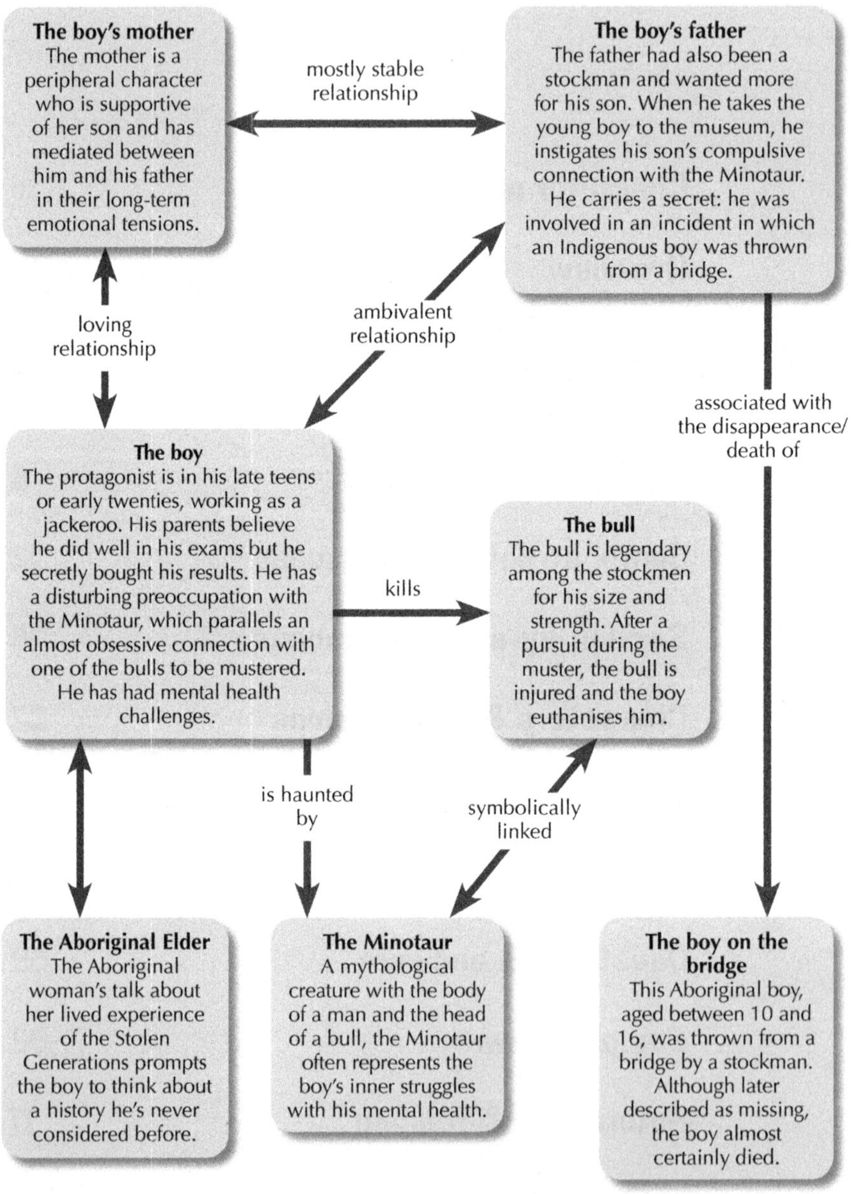

OVERVIEW

Note: While it is vital to consider the appropriateness of particular terms when describing aspects of First Nations culture, there are not always simple 'right' choices. This guide uses two terms from the text, Aboriginal and Indigenous, in addition to the widely accepted term 'First Nations'. In general, 'Indigenous' should be capitalised when referring to First Nations peoples and cultures. However, *Requiem for a Beast* uses a lower case i for 'indigenous' and that convention is retained in quotations from the text. Similarly, although the text uses lower case e for 'elder', this guide capitalises 'Elder' when referring to First Nations people, including characters in the text.

About the author

Matt Ottley is a writer, painter, illustrator, musician and composer. He was born in 1962 in Papua New Guinea where his Australian parents were living. His family moved back to Australia in 1974 when the traumatic and unsafe personal and political landscape in Papua New Guinea became untenable. Although Australia was safer at the time, Ottley did not escape some of his personal demons, and at times he felt very alienated in his new context and life – experiences that have made their way into some of his books.

Requiem for a Beast was published in 2007 and the following year was awarded the Children's Book Council of Australia (CBCA) Picture Book of the Year and the Queensland Premier's Literary Award for Best Young Adult Book. Although it is not an autobiography, the text includes many elements that reflect aspects of Ottley's own life, including battles with mental health and his relationship with his father. Ottley witnessed racism like that in the book, while working on a cattle station in Queensland after failing high school, and, like the boy in *Requiem for a Beast*, struggled with his mental health. Following that, he began to focus on his music and his art, until his mental health declined again; he then spent many years alternating between outback stations and urban life. As a young adult he combined these experiences and established a career in the UK as a specialist painter of horses – this clearly provided a background for his detailed horse imagery in *Requiem for a Beast*.

Interestingly for a visual artist, Ottley is red-green colourblind, and also a synaesthete: someone who involuntarily experiences relationships between various sensory stimuli. In Ottley's synaesthesia, he experiences sound as colour. It is interesting to consider the influence synaesthesia might have on Ottley's creation of multimodal works; he has noted that '*Requiem for a Beast* has cloud shapes that come out of what I see when I hear the opening string music I wrote for that work' (Lawn 2022).

Ottley has contributed to more than twenty books, often as sole author and illustrator (and sometimes composer also), but also as the illustrator for other writers' works. *Requiem for a Beast* was his first major multimodal work for an older audience, and has been followed by others including *The Tree of Ecstasy and Unbearable Sadness* (2022).

Synopsis

Requiem for a Beast is a complex multimodal work comprising not only multiple literary modes but also a short musical chamber work. Within these broad modes, there are yet more mediums of storytelling. The literary component is constructed of many modal 'voices', such as first-person and third-person narratives, wordless graphic panel sequences, a speech and an extract from a museum display. Fonts and layouts vary and sometimes textual watermarks (both Latin and Bundjalung) are included behind text. The audio component is also composed of multiple 'voices': it is written for a chamber ensemble and two vocalists, and includes Latin and Bundjalung lyrics, and sometimes English spoken word. These threads of aural narrative are also enriched by various allusions, such as to the traditional religious verse, the Requiem. Structurally, the book is divided into five parts, each named for a movement of the Requiem, with the fifth section being the musical piece itself.

The central story of the book is that of 'the boy', a young adult who works as a jackeroo (similar to an apprentice) on a rural Australian cattle station. Having finished school and deferred his university degree, the boy has gone to work on a station because his school results, which his father described as 'brilliant' (p.20), were in fact a lie, and he does not feel that he can fulfil the bright future his parents expect of him. By going to work as a station hand, the boy is disappointing his father, not only because he seems to be throwing away a better career, but also due to the father's own ghosts from his past as a ringer (cattle worker). In particular, the boy's father carries a secret that tears him up from the inside until he is compelled to tell it to the boy's mother: while working as a ringer, he was a passenger in a vehicle while a mate harassed and (almost certainly) killed a young Indigenous boy. It was never spoken of by the men, and the father has been plagued by guilt for many years. The boy, overhearing the story, becomes burdened by some of this guilt and sadness, and it merges with his own guilt about having 'bought' his school results (p.62); his ambivalent relationship with his father; and, more deeply, his powerful struggles against his own abstract fears.

These fears, associated with his fragile mental health (which in turn leads to a suicide attempt – an event not explored explicitly in the text), become inextricably intertwined with the myth of the Minotaur, which becomes for him a strange hybrid of torment and temptation. Ultimately, the boy follows and attempts to catch a bull that seems to represent the Minotaur, and when it is mortally injured he sees no option but to kill it. He is devastated by his own part in its death.

An additional narrative thread is that of the boy's growing awareness of Indigenous dispossession at the hands of white colonisers and contemporary white Australia, and the devastation this has wrought on the country's First Peoples. When en route to his job at the station, he happens upon a talk by an Aboriginal Elder at a community hall and hears firsthand of tragedies he knew nothing about, including the experiences of the Stolen Generations and the lasting damage and trauma resulting from this.

In the boy's head, all these events and ideas – the murder of the boy on the bridge, the history of the Stolen Generations, his own psychological distress, mythical beasts, his father's imperfections and the pursuit of the wild bull – become enmeshed and inseparable, culminating in the killing of the bull.

The structural position of the book's denouement is held by the fifth and final section of the work, the Requiem musical composition. This, too, is divided into sections, each movement named for a verse of the traditional Latin Requiem. The composition, for small chamber orchestra and vocalists, draws into the narrative of the book the grief of a requiem and of a number of traditional First Nations songs. The music, which ranges from discordant and percussive to melodically cinematic, in its own way tells the story of the rest of the book (although it is not written as a 'soundtrack').

The book contains much ambiguity, many layers of overlapping and tangled symbolism, abstract ideas and elliptical thought, leaving room for interpretation regarding the actual 'plot' itself, as well the boy's inner experience. However, concrete events (such as the visit to the museum, the death of the bull and the incident with the boy on the bridge) guide interpretations to focus on key themes of grief, fear and struggle.

Character summaries

The boy

The unnamed protagonist is in his late teens or early twenties. He works on a cattle station as a jackeroo after deferring his university studies. He is haunted by a huge bull he links to the mythological Minotaur, with whom he has a confused connection; he seems to believe that it is somehow his destiny to merge with or conquer the bull. The boy is troubled and struggles with mental health challenges.

The boy's parents

The boy's mother is a sympathetic character who sends him books to read on the station, and who in the boy's younger days often bridged gaps between the boy and his father. The boy's father is a complex character who has ambivalent feelings about his own past life as a ringer and therefore does not want his son to follow in his footsteps (though is still brought alive by the rose-tinted memories of those times).

The bull

The bull is both a literal beast involved in the muster (a round-up of livestock) and also a symbol of the boy's own mental and emotional struggles. After escaping the previous year's muster, when he killed a man, the bull is caught and killed by the boy.

The stockmen

These ringers work alongside the boy during cattle-mustering season. Although each of the stockmen is (unlike the boy) named, there is little difference in the roles they play in the text, and all are relatively minor characters. They include Pete, Rudy and Johnno.

The boy on the bridge

Aged somewhere between ten and sixteen, the Indigenous boy was murdered years ago while the protagonist's father was a passenger in a car. He often appears in the protagonist's dreams and imagination.

Note: To avoid confusion, this guide refers to this character as 'the boy on the bridge' and the protagonist as 'the boy'.

The Aboriginal Elder

This Aboriginal Elder gives a speech at a community hall that the boy attends; she discusses the Stolen Generations and her own lived experience. She becomes central to the boy's emotional journey.

BACKGROUND & CONTEXT

Author's context: mental health

Matt Ottley has described elements of the book as autobiographical, and the boy's experience as a jackeroo on a cattle station is drawn from Ottley's own time as a stationman. This was a job he returned to again and again, despite being plagued by some of the same psychological traumas portrayed in the boy's story. Although Ottley has spoken and written elsewhere about mental health issues needing to be acknowledged openly and compassionately, and has discussed his own struggles with bipolar disorder, the psychological issues faced by the boy in *Requiem for a Beast* are not explicitly identified.

This guide describes the boy's mental health struggle as being depression; the occasional textual references (and the illustration on p.62) suggest that this is likely what he has suffered from. The boy describes the 'beast' (referring to the Minotaur, but also to the psychological 'beast' that plagues him) as something that 'hunted' and 'tracked' him through the years, slowly draining his 'spirit' from him 'until there was nothing left' and it 'almost took [him]' (p.63). This image echoes the colloquial analogy of clinical depression as a 'black dog' that follows a person.

Ottley's book has been criticised (sometimes by readers or reviewers who did not understand the target age group of the book) for including references to suicide. The first is when the boy empathises with his parents' 'finding me on my bed, almost gone' after apparently attempting suicide with the pills beside his bed (p.21). The second is when the Aboriginal Elder speaks of her sister, who tried to 'belt the memory out of [herself] ... with alcohol' (p.43), and dies in the hospital like so many other 'stolen people' who 'drank themselves to death' (p.44).

Cultural context

Ottley has said of his multimodal work, 'I love the idea of referencing the complex connectedness of different, often disparate cultural ideas and modalities that make up any single cultural expression' (Lawn 2022). In *Requiem for a Beast*, part of this 'complex connectedness' involves not only harnessing many narrative modes in the storytelling (such as images and music), but also drawing on a wider repertoire of narrative and artistic forms, implicitly connecting the boy's story to broader ideas.

Religious allusions

Although there is no explicit exploration of religion in the textual narrative of the story, the section titles are drawn from sections of a Roman Catholic Requiem.

A requiem is a religious mass for the dead, and can also describe the setting of such a service to music, or a service, poem or song composed in commemoration of the soul of a person who has died. The term is also sometimes appropriated for secular and/or less formal ceremonies or musical works. The Latin words to the specific musical requiem written for *Requiem for a Beast* are extracted from a traditional Roman Catholic liturgical sequence composed sometime in the thirteenth century. Other well-known musical settings of parts of this same text include Mozart's *Requiem in D minor* in the late eighteenth century and, in a more modern example, Andrew Lloyd Webber's *Requiem* composed in the 1980s. By shaping his book around this particular Latin verse, Ottley alludes to the rich history of the requiem form and its many centuries of adaptation. The book reminds readers that the present is always built on the past.

Ottley himself has described his motivations for incorporating the Requiem:

> ... at heart the original Requiem is about the grieving process, about resolution and finding peace. I thought this

> was appropriate given the story of the Stolen Generations coupled with the theme of a dysfunctional masculine culture underlying much of contemporary Australian society. The Aboriginal stories contain themes that either work in tandem with those of the Latin text, or work thematically in an ironic way. (Lawn 2022)

Musical allusions

Although the music written for the text is contemporary in style, the arrangement itself is reasonably conventional and the instruments are all traditional classical instruments that might be found in an orchestra. The introduction of the storytelling as a spoken-word component (the Bundjalung-speaking man who narrates in English some of the songs' content) is less usual, and exemplifies the way that Ottley works with many different narrative modes and threads throughout this text.

As with the use of the Requiem text, the allusions to historical art forms is a reminder that texts and ideas cannot exist without the context of earlier work. Few textual themes are ever unique; rather, it is the way they are combined and explored that creates meaning in a text.

Classical mythology

The text draws on Greek mythology to incorporate bigger stories and wider themes that reflect or illuminate characters and ideas in the book. Greek and Roman mythology, as with the lore of many other religions and cultures, was a way for the ancient Greeks and Romans to hand down origin stories. Myths were often shared not just orally but also through representations in art and other mediums such as decorative and functional pottery vessels and other physical artefacts. In this sense, the myths themselves are multimodal, so it seems fitting that they form some of the narrative threads in Ottley's multimodal work.

Many of these myths have been documented, explored and retold by artists over the intervening centuries, and while we do not know if the stories were interpreted literally by their originators, certainly now we read them as symbolic of various human qualities, relationships and challenges to be faced. This is the mode in which Ottley uses myth in *Requiem for a Beast* – as examination of non-literal aspects of the world.

The myth of the Minotaur plays a significant role in the boy's life. Encountering the story during a museum visit as a child, he becomes preoccupied with the Minotaur, later conflating it with the bull and with his own personal struggles. That the museum visit is associated with several other incidents in that same week is also significant. There are three particular events that the boy relates as part of the central story of the Minotaur:

- overhearing his father chatting with an old ringer mate, and hearing the man's extremely racist judgements
- not having a chance to ask his father to help him fix up his old toy
- attempting to reach out for friendship but being aggressively rejected by the popular new boy at school.

These three events, when correlated with his visit to the museum, create a complex, layered series of ideas and character development, and even the boy himself is unable to articulate what the relationship between the events and his connection to the Minotaur might have been. He only knows that 'something extraordinary – something profound – lodged itself inside me' (p.60), and for the rest of his life he will connect that emotional awakening with the Minotaur and, by extension, with the Brahmin bull.

The myth of the centaur, while not as central to the boy's story, is still an important underlying image and idea. As with the Minotaur, the centaur is a creature that is half animal and half human – specifically, half horse, which is relevant in terms of the connection the boy later makes with horses. It also reiterates the idea presented by the Minotaur myth, that humans and animals are much more closely connected than we might at first believe. Although the book only provides us with a brief overview of the creatures, it is enough to hint at some of the ideas the boy takes away with him from the museum that day.

In case his readers are not familiar with Greek mythology, on page 61 Ottley provides an overview, in the style of a museum's interpretive material (which the boy and his father appear to be reading at the museum, in one of the panels on the facing page).

First Nations context

Although Ottley is a non-Indigenous Australian, he worked closely with a number of individuals and communities to connect to the language he chose to include in his composition. In his 'Notes on the CD', he mentions that, although the language used in the recording is that of the Bundjalung Nation, a single First Nations language can comprise numerous dialects and links with other nearby languages.

He also notes that he has not specifically situated the book in any particular part of Australia, but rather that it could take place in various remote or rural locations. This suggests that he wants his narrative to encompass much wider stories – even though it focuses on a single protagonist – and not be tied to the experiences of a particular community or nation. The Aboriginal Elder, for example, speaks of her own family's trauma caused by the government removing children from their families and communities. But her story is representative of many: she says that her sister's tragedy 'was a common story' (p.43) and she wants her audience to understand both the personal impact and the widespread trauma resulting from these policies and actions.

It is important also to situate the text within the time line of recognition of past crimes against the original inhabitants of this country, and the need for and journey towards reconciliation. Note, for example, that the book was published ten years after the 'Bringing them Home' report tabled in Parliament in 1997. This report summarised the work of the two-year-long National Inquiry into the Separation of Aboriginal and Torres Strait Islander Children from Their Families, conducted by what was then the Human Rights and Equal Opportunity Commission. The report explored the details of forced removal policies and the lasting impacts on those taken, including issues of intergenerational trauma and grief. It also included many individual stories of the kind that the Aboriginal Elder tells in Part Two of this text, as well as proposing means for reparation, reconciliation, support and healing going forward.

Subsequent events in a long journey towards reconciliation include the introduction of Sorry Day in 1998, the reconciliation bridge walks in 2000, and in 2008 (the same year *Requiem for a Beast* won the CBCA award), Prime Minister Kevin Rudd's formal apology speech to Australia's Indigenous communities, with particular reference to the Stolen Generations (Rudd 2008). While these events are not explicitly acknowledged in the text, they are important contextual elements to consider in relation to the events and attitudes in the text and the cultural and social environment in which Ottley was writing.

GENRE, STRUCTURE & LANGUAGE

Genre

Requiem for a Beast is a complex multimodal text in which even the primary modes (image, text and music) contain multiple 'voices'. Although it is often marketed as a picture book, the text contains elements drawn from a variety of genres. Features that combine to tell the story include:

- a graphic-novel format
- full-page illustrations
- handwriting-style text (first person), and changing font and formatting styles
- traditional third-person text/narrative
- a speech transcript
- dream sequences and flashbacks
- informational/educational interpretive material at a museum
- chamber music in both contemporary and classical styles (including operatic solo and traditional Indigenous songs)
- spoken-word storytelling
- Latin, English and Bundjalung text, speech and song.

From each of the genres or subgenres the text takes various features and combines them into a generally coherent narrative – although there are many instances where what is being communicated is so symbolic and abstract as to be very open to individual interpretation. All of these elements together form what is in fact a fairly conventional plot – a concentrated and heavily symbolic coming-of-age journey – though it is conveyed in an unconventional form.

Varied generic features often work together, as in the following examples.

- Narrative text boxes may accompany panel sequences, describing literally what is happening.
- The Latin translations and the Bundjalung translations directly accompany the song cycle.
- Full-page images use colour to convey mood and tone.
- Font and formatting often represent voice or mode (such as the italics for the Elder's speech, or the coloured font connected to the disturbing beast, p.15).

Remember that you will be analysing the text as a whole and, while it is important to identify and understand the genres contributing to its construction, what is most important is that you are able to analyse and discuss the ways in which all these features work *together* to construct meaning.

Structure

Note that many of the pages (those dominated by images or panels) are not visibly numbered, making it sometimes difficult to locate text, images or incidents you may want to analyse or quote. It is useful to mark pages with bookmarks or sticky tabs to identify sections and page numbers, or to mark pages containing events significant for your analysis (for example, the key museum information about the centaurs and Minotaur appears on p.61).

Plot events

The plot itself is divided into segments and often interrupted by flashbacks, but the point in the plot's time line to which a section refers is usually clear. This may be indicated by demonstrating the boy's age, such as in the museum section, where the images of him and the concrete events that concern him – his toy and the party – distinctly portray a young boy; or in the single-page image of the boy as an older student (p.62), where he has clearly aged physically, and the computer's text document reflected in the window behind him indicates that the image takes place after the boy's schooling.

The plot of *Requiem for a Beast* can be broken down into the following chronological series of key events.

- The father, a ringer, is implicated in and a witness to the event with the boy on the bridge.
- As a child, the boy decided to give his beloved toy plane to another child at school to impress him.
- Intending to ask his father to help with the plane, the boy overhears him talking to an ex-ringer mate who uses aggressive and offensive racist language.
- The boy attends the party with his gift (the plane) and is rejected.
- The father takes the boy to the museum.
- The boy's father tells his mother the terrible story of the boy on the bridge.
- The boy fails at school, but cheats by buying good results.
- The boy attempts suicide.
- The boy travels to a town to be collected for his new job as a jackeroo.
- The boy attends a talk by an Aboriginal Elder.
- The boy works on the mustering station.
- The boy hunts/tracks and ultimately kills the bull.

While many of the plot 'events' (such as those above) are concrete, the text includes a number of dreams and memories. As a result, some details of the plot are symbolic and figurative, and it is likely that you will interpret parts of this text very subjectively.

Chronology

Due to its multimodal form, the chronological structure of the text is extremely complex. Even flashbacks are not straightforward. Events and time frames overlap, such as when the boy is catching the bull while his father – in the boy's memory, in his past – describes the incident with the boy on the bridge. Dream sequences, such as in the early pages or on pages 51–5, interrupt the chronological progression of events, and may reflect events and ideas that occur either earlier in the text or later (or even both). Some events remain suspended in an unspecified time frame, and some elements stand outside the time frame, such as the character list identifying all the ringers (pp.24–5). Other parts of the time frame are internally consistent and chronological (such as when the boy arrives in the town and then listens to the old woman's talk, pp.40–5); but, even at times when the boy is telling a single story, he may shift back and forth in time, such as in the story of the birthday party and the museum, when the narrative interrupts itself to say, 'anyway, I'm jumping the gun' (p.57).

At the same time, however, the broad structure of the text is very concrete and carefully constructed. The book is divided into four distinct narrative parts (Parts One to Four), creating clear distinctions in the story, as well as Part Five (the musical element). Equally, the musical score is separated into four movements (with the same names as the part names in the written text).

Language

As a multimodal text, *Requiem for a Beast* employs a wide range of language techniques. Not only are different 'languages' used to create the text (verbal, visual and musical), but within each of these, many specific language features are employed, creating – just as in a conventional written text – mood, tone and meaning, and helping to develop themes and characters.

Textual language

The written text is mainly in English, although the cover pages for each chapter contain watermark text in either Latin or Bundjalung. The lyrics from the musical composition are also presented in Part Five, where both the Latin and Bundjalung songs are transcribed and accompanied by an English translation.

The different narrative voices – the third-person and first-person sections – vary a little in register, with the protagonist's first-person perspective using a more informal vocabulary, and sometimes speaking almost directly to the reader, as in 'yes, he rose to the top pretty quickly if I remember rightly' (p.56). The third-person sections, on the other hand, tend to use more formal constructions and are often descriptive and poetic, contributing to the dreamlike tone of the text. Figurative language is often used to create tone, mood and imagery. Examples of this include the following.

- Personification: 'The country is hunched against the heat, tormented by the promise of rain' (p.56).
- Sensory imagery: 'The smell of sweat rises from the darkened shoulders of the mare, mixing with the musky scent of leather, and the pearly smell of coming rain' (p.64); 'lightning suddenly splits the sky white, and a second later thunder explodes across the landscape' (p.76).
- Simile: 'its hump rolls slightly to one side and then back, like the opening and closing of a boxer's fist' (p.64); 'the beast-man is circling the building like a lion, purring, growling' (p.13).

In some sections the language is carefully concrete and detailed, creating a clear narrative recount of events, such as the muster in Part One, while at other times the focus is on emotive language that prompts powerful responses in readers, such as in the description of the bull's death, or in the language the Elder uses to tell her story.

Visual language

The visual imagery in *Requiem for a Beast* relies on traditional conventions of illustrative art, such as choice of colour palette and composition, and also harnesses many conventions more specific to graphic novels, such as the use of panels, borders, gutters (space between panels) and text boxes. Although containing many different visual styles – including sweeping, nightmarish dream spreads; pencil drawings; and simple boxed images – the illustrations always reflect some part of the text, pairing to tell the story. When analysing visual elements, consider how they combine with the written text to create tone or mood or to convey meaning, as in the following examples.

- The handwritten style of the first-person narrative helps to convey the very personal nature of the boy's thoughts.
- The full-page images (such as of the father on the horse, p.19, or the boy at his computer, p.62) emphasise the importance of characters or events.
- The panels that zoom in on the Elder's eyes (p.42) reflect the way that her story is giving the boy a close insight into her experiences.
- The dark backgrounds throughout the Rudy dream (pp.51–5) help create the dark emotional tone of this dream.

Musical language

You do not need to have a specialist knowledge of musical conventions and terms in order to discuss this text (if you are expected to discuss the music as a part of the text at all). You can discuss the music even in very simple terms, such as whether a particular section is fast/slow, loud/soft, high/low. This will allow you to identify the contribution made by the music to the overall narrative of the text. For example, the middle of the Dies Irae movement becomes quite fast, complicated and climactic, which echoes the boy's nightmare.

SECTION-BY-SECTION ANALYSIS

Cover and front matter

Although not traditionally considered part of a narrative, the front cover of this text is where the visual storytelling begins, and it offers you quick practice in interpreting the illustrative content of the book. The menacing, mournful mood of the text is captured in the dark palette and the looming storm clouds. While the figures are static, standing almost calmly beside each other, there is a strong sense of foreboding created by the intense shadows and low contrast. The figures are the (literal) beast of the title, and a young Indigenous boy, giving us a hint at some of the ideas explored in the text, such as the history of the Stolen Generations and the complex relationships between humans and animals. The watermarked echo of the title words also hints at the important relationship between text and image throughout the book.

Q Why do you think the cover image does not feature the protagonist?

Part One: Dies Irae (pp.1–38)

Summary: *Landscape is visually established in panels; the boy has a nightmare during which he warns an Indigenous boy to run from a schoolyard as a man approaches; the man turns into a beast; the boy prepares for the day of muster at a cattle station; the boy reflects on having followed his father into station work; the boy remembers his parents finding him alive after a suicide attempt; all the station men are introduced; the muster begins; the boy comes face to face with the bull.*

The book begins with a double-page spread of a landscape and skyscape, with the phrase, 'It's our memories that make us' (p.2). This is deliberately presented entirely out of context: we don't yet know who the narrator is, what landscape is portrayed, whose memories might be relevant or how this relates to the story to come. However, as with the imagery and words on the cover, tone and ideas are immediately suggested. The colour palette in the landscape is dark and brooding, with mainly blues, greens and greys and little warmth. The landscape's vastness and the dominance of the stormy sky suggest the insignificance of humankind within the natural world. Paired with this image, the words initiate a sense of the progression of time and the influence of the past in the present. Later these ideas will connect with the Aboriginal woman's history as well as with the protagonist, who is plagued by his own memories and the past experiences that he feels have 'haunted [his] dreams since childhood' (p.22). The subsequent full-spread pages and large panels with sparse text contribute to the establishment of a very dark reality – literally, in terms of colour, and figuratively, in terms of fear and loss (the words are from the Aboriginal Elder's later speech about the Stolen Generations).

When the main written text begins, it draws on the landscape imagery that preceded it, but it is in a traditionally formatted black typeface on white pages. This contrast between pages is stark; throughout the book, text and imagery tend to be more integrated. While the text is descriptive, detailed and vivid, it begins in medias res (in the middle of things) so it is still not clear who the bull or the boy are, or where the story is set other than a 'flood plain' somewhere (p.9). The boy himself seems vague about his surroundings. He dreams he is in a place that 'he knows ... but can't remember from where'; it is 'a place imbued with a feeling he can't quite name' (p.9). Just like a dream, everything seems patchy and mysterious, setting the tone for much of the rest of the text.

Key point

Part One of the text places enormous demands on the reader: we are presented with much information through the multiple narrative voices and visual styles, yet little that is solid or easy to grasp. Just when one thing seems explicit, the form of text or the style of illustration shifts entirely, leaving us uncertain again about how to piece the elements together into a cohesive narrative.

In another initially jarring shift, pages 10 and 11 present a double spread of illustrated panels against a black background and with a single line of text, as we see the unidentified scene through the boy's eyes. Over the next few pages, as the dream becomes a nightmare, the illustrative style shifts again, now into a much more urgent and fractured panel layout, while the narrative point of view shifts too, into the first-person voice of the protagonist. The first emotional climax occurs on pages 14 and 15, when the boy's dream concludes with the hideous beast – a man-turned-Minotaur – smashing into the schoolroom. These two pages use various visual techniques to enhance the disturbing impact of what is being described verbally. Vivid, violent words such as 'crack', 'smashed' (p.14), 'throws', 'screams' and 'roars' (p.15) accompany the horrific imagery. On one page, the beast is shown in shadowy sections of body parts, split across shattered pieces of a single panel, the illustration broken just as the wall is broken by the beast, and the boy's safety is shattered in his dream. The next page provides a startling contrast: the fully formed frightening head of the beast, with piercing teeth and horn, tongue lolling and saliva drooling. The background to this page is a bold red, as is the text in the ragged-edged text box. The use of the colour red, alongside sharp edges and dark shadowy forms, connotes the anger, danger and fear associated with the beast. This kind of emotion, we later understand, has haunted the boy since childhood. Ideas and events referenced in these early pages will later have meaning.

Key point

Red is used rarely in the text, especially in this quantity and vividness (another use is on page 23, which echoes this page). By using the colour sparingly, Ottley increases its emotional impact through contrast with the dominant palette.

Following the intense opening to the book, from page 16 the narrative becomes more concrete, introducing us to the boy's life on the station, as the men prepare for the day's muster. The serif typeface (one in which the letters are embellished with small lines at the base and top), here in black on white, will be the one used throughout the text when the story is being told in the third person. (The corresponding italic font later represents the Aboriginal Elder's speech.) The cursive or handwriting-style typeface represents the boy's first-person recounts throughout. The differences allow us to distinguish the multiple voices through which the text is constructed, and are an example of how a literary feature (narrative perspective) is paired with a visual feature (typesetting) to construct meaning. While at times the font colours shift (determined by the colour of the image or panel behind the text), for the majority of the book the block font is in white or black, while the cursive font is in a pale tan. This general consistency helps guide readers through the complex multi-voiced narrative.

The text narrative between pages 16 and 25 is a more conventionally expository section. Despite the stockmen being only minor characters, each of them is introduced in detail (pp.24–5). We learn a little of the boy's background, such as the fact that he is following in his father's footsteps working on stations, and also the fact that his father had not wanted his son to carry on that legacy, particularly as he believes his son's academic results are outstanding. The boy's doleful thought, 'if only his father knew the truth about those school results' (p.20) foreshadows a later event: when we learn that the boy cheated and 'bought' those results (p.62).

Another significant introduction here is 'that bull' (p.18) – a bull famed for escaping muster and nearly killing a man. For some reason this bull has lodged itself in the boy's consciousness and, even though the head stockman has warned his crew that if any of them see the bull, they should 'leave it' for him to shoot (p.18), there is already a hint that the boy would like to tackle it himself. Perhaps he imagines this will make the others on the station finally respect him as a ringer or perhaps he hopes to vanquish his own personal demons; the motif of the bull carries the boy's darker and more complex preoccupation with the mythical Minotaur.

On page 21 the narrative indelibly links the murder of the boy on the bridge, the deep and lasting scars of colonisation (and particularly the realities of the Stolen Generations), and the boy's own attempted suicide. For the boy, as for his father, these stories become tangled and somehow merge with the myth of the Minotaur: page 23 shows the boy morphing into a Minotaur himself, in a confused blend of his own mental trauma and the role he thinks he plays in his father's mind.

Q What did you think the book was about, from your first reading of this section?

Q How would you describe the boy?

Key vocabulary

Brahmin (also sometimes 'Brahman'): a particular breed of beef cattle in Australia (originally from India), developed to tolerate a hot climate.

Centaur: a Greek mythological creature, part human and part horse.

Dies Irae: a Latin phrase meaning day of wrath.

Jackeroo (usually spelled 'jackaroo'): a young man working on a sheep or cattle station to gain experience – similar to an apprentice.

Minotaur: a Greek mythological creature, part human and part bull.

Muster: gather; in this context the word specifically refers to the rounding-up of cattle (many of whom may be wild) around a rural cattle station, by workers on horseback.

Ringer: a stock worker or cattle drover.

Yang-yang: a description of a horse that is troublesome or spirited.

Part Two: Mors Stupebit et Natura (pp.39–46)

Summary: *The boy travels to town to be picked up by the head stockman for his new job at a cattle station; he attends a talk by an Aboriginal Elder in the community hall; she tells the story of her own and her siblings' experiences as children of the Stolen Generations.*

The story shifts back in time, as the boy arrives at the town where Johnno, the head stockman, will collect him for his job on the station. The wordless panels show the boy travelling by bus across wide brown landscapes into a small quiet town. When, by chance, he strolls past the community hall, he is drawn to a photograph or drawing of a group of Indigenous children. The close-up of this image contrasts its stark black-and-white palette with the dusty colours of the highway and the town (p.41), indicating the importance of this new element of the story. The boy enters the hall and listens to the Aboriginal Elder's story about the Stolen Generations. The boy, who has 'never really given much thought to indigenous people' (p.17), joins readers in bearing witness to the woman's trauma. Hers is the only voice in this short section, as she relates her own and her sister's experiences of being taken from their families, raised in homes, then left disconnected from their own societies – some Stolen Generations children were so damaged by this that they later committed suicide.

Key point

The woman's story includes an anecdote about a teacher helping children escape classrooms, wanting to 'save them from being taken' (p.44). This is retrospectively echoed in the dream in the opening pages, when the protagonist helps a young Indigenous boy out of a window to escape the approaching man (who then becomes the monstrous beast). This story, like the myths of the centaurs and Minotaur, lodges itself in the boy's mind, manifests in his dreams and becomes tangled with other stories.

Pages 43 to 45 contain text but no illustrations, leaving the visual images of the woman's story to readers' own imaginations. This creates a strong contrast with the intense, wordless images at the end of the previous section, when the panels zoomed in on the bull's and the Indigenous boy's eyes. While containing only text, however, these three pages still make use of visual design, with some paragraphs offset and isolated from others, surrounded by more than the usual amount of white space. Also, watermarked behind the main text are the Bundjalung words to the song 'Ghost Story' from Pie Jesu (p.88). Thus, while there is only a single 'voice' on the page here, the text is still calling in the 'ghosts' of others: literally, here, the song of the man who performs in this hall after the woman (a song also included in the musical component of the text). The song tells a historical story, of an Indigenous man first seeing white people and horses, interpreting them as two-headed beasts, which calls to mind the double nature of the Minotaur and the centaurs.

Key point

Note that although the text in this chapter is in the same typeface as the third-person sections of the boy's narrative elsewhere, it is inflected by being presented in italics, thus is technically a new font, so that the same typeface can incorporate a new narrative voice.

Q The final paragraph shifts to a figurative use of language that contrasts strongly with the concrete language of the rest of the section. What are the effects of this?

Key vocabulary

Mors Stupebit et Natura: a Latin phrase translated in this text as 'death and nature will be stupefied' (p.86).

Stolen people: members of the Stolen Generations (First Nations children forcibly removed from their families over many decades).

The missions: reserves based around churches and run by church officials and missionaries (sometimes with government involvement), to which First Nations people were relocated in the 1800s and early 1900s.

Part Three: Lacrymosa (pp.47–72)

Summary: *The boy, on horseback, follows the bull; the boy recalls his dream about Rudy turning into a Minotaur and about an Aboriginal woman who has lost a child; he recalls going to a party as a child and being rejected; he recalls his father taking him to the museum, where he first learned about the Minotaur; the father tells the story of the boy on the bridge; the bull and the boy fall off a cliff.*

Time shifts forward again to take up from where Part One left off: with horse, boy and bull in a stand-off in a 'small clearing, a natural amphitheatre' (p.32). Abruptly, instead of attacking, the bull turns and leaves and, just as in his dream in Part One, the boy is compelled to follow. In that dream, the boy 'knows this place, but can't remember from where' (p.9), and he feels similarly now. The dreamscape and landscape overlap, and reality becomes dreamlike, as the boy is filled with a 'sense of desperation' that he must not lose the bull (p.50). Far from being a high-tension chase, however, the bull leads at a walk and the boy follows, as if mesmerised, 'slowly through the glaring heat, deeper into the day and deeper into himself' (p.50).

There is a suspenseful, surreal, existential tone to the moment, and it leads the boy to reflect back on another dream he experienced in the same landscape – although visually it is strikingly different. The sun-bleached yellows of the wide plains of his first dream have been replaced by claustrophobic deep blues and blacks, the termite hills transitioning into nightmarish toxic-green protuberances. The contrast between these two landscapes might be seen as representing a contrast between an inner and an outer life for the boy – what he feels versus what he presents to the world. In this dream, confused ideas torment the boy as Rudy, one of the Indigenous ringers, begins to tame a horse but is soon merged with it instead, to become a 'hideous screaming' Minotaur (p.53). Accompanying this frightening transition is Rudy's terrified cry, 'Please don't take me away' (p.52), a clear echo of the Indigenous boy in the first dream, and of the Aboriginal Elder's story of being taken. She, too, or perhaps a younger version of her (her pink top is the same colour as the woman's shirt in the community hall) appears in this nightmare.

After the dream, as the boy continues to follow the bull, we witness several key scenes from his childhood, which help us begin to draw connections between some of the erratic images and moments shown so far. First is the boy's rejection by a fellow schoolchild, which initially seems a simple childish pain. But in the boy's mind it is intertwined with the complexities of his relationship with his father, and with the visit from his father's old ringer mate, whose casual racism disrupts the family's stability. In turn, the boy associates this event with his father not being there to support him, since he feels retrospectively that his father could have helped with repairing the toy plane, preventing the boy's embarrassment and rejection at the party. The second significant event occurs the day after the party and is the visit to the museum, where the Greek myths, most particularly that of the Minotaur, for no logical reason take up enduring residence in the boy's mind.

Key point

Note how the text and image on page 61 are differentiated from other sections of the book. The typeface here is a sans serif font, a type of font often used in situations where clarity of communication is key, such as in online or formal documents. As well as differentiating this informational 'voice' from the rest of the text, the choice of font here helps make the event stand out, indicating its significance and importance for the boy.

The text suggests that, to the boy, the Minotaur represents his own inner demons – his fears, his feelings of rejection and abandonment, and his depression. Quickly these demons escalate, and the next thing we learn is that the boy 'bought' his school results (p.62). The full-page illustration shows the boy, tormented, at his computer where he has typed a message to his parents to tell them about the results. However, we see the text not from his point of view but rather reflected in a mirror beside him. Thus the text is backwards, representing his inner turmoil, the depth of his unbearable secret and the difficulty of exorcising it. Further, the mirror is also reflecting the Minotaur looking in at the boy through a window; both the words and the Minotaur loom over the boy, hunched at his desk.

However, the next thing the boy reveals is that, although his demons, embodied in the Minotaur, have 'hunted', 'tracked' and 'pursued' him through the years, he also feels that the beast has been a positive motivator for him, something 'beautiful, powerful, desirable' that has kept him reaching forward (p.63). This reflects the way that the bull during the muster is not chasing him but instead drawing him on. And as that journey continues across the plains, he is suddenly reminded of the story of the boy on the bridge. The next section (pp.65–9) offers two simultaneous narratives: one, in the image boxes at the outer edges of the pages, is the boy finally catching the bull by the tail, and the other, in the central two-thirds of each page, is the father's story of the boy on the bridge. The capture of the bull is wordless, while the words of the father's story pour out.

Key point

The boy and his father both wear green shirts in these panels, forcing us to draw parallels between them, each haunted by their past. Likewise, they are linked by the similar images of them in despair, miserably holding their hands over their faces (the boy, p.62, and the father, pp.66–7).

The overlap between the two stories is intricate and complex, as ideas of guilt, masculinity/manhood, strength, battle, choice, shame and death all assault the reader, tangled through generational memory and trauma. The stories climax together as the boy draws the bull to the edge of a cliff and, on page 69, all the threads of the text come together in a cascade of panels and textboxes portraying:

- the Aboriginal Elder mourning her sister
- the young protagonist longing for his father's help
- the father haunted by the story of the boy on the bridge
- the Elder's sister being beaten
- the boy's foot slipping at the edge of the embankment.

As the boy and bull fall, the section concludes with a page of white text on black, and two surreal pages featuring the masked rider from the first dream; an axe dripping blood; a giant Minotaur morphing into darkness and clouds; and a young Indigenous boy clinging to the end of a rope. As in the dream sections, these pages are not intended to be read literally, so you need to look instead for symbolism in order to build an interpretation of what these pages tell you about the narrative. Below are some possible interpretations.

- In the text, the bull 'wrenches him around in another attempt to horn him' (p.70), an image representing the longevity of the boy's battle with his mental health.
- The axe dripping blood (p.71) could symbolise colonial genocide, the boy's attempts to slay his inner own demon, or the death of the boy on the bridge (or more than one of these).
- The Minotaur and the darkness/clouds merging together might represent the all-consuming nature of trauma and grief.
- The images of ropes relate to the literal situation of a stockman catching a bull. But they also allude to the restrictions the boy's traumas have placed on his life and the way Indigenous children have been held largely captive (as in missions).

Q What do you consider to be the strongest image in this section (verbal or visual), and why?

Key vocabulary

Jins: an offensive and dated slang term for Aboriginal women.

Lacrymosa: a Latin word meaning weeping or tearful.

Piccaninnies: an offensive and dated term for dark-skinned children.

Sophistry: falseness.

Part Four: Pie Jesu (pp.73–82)

Summary: *The boy regains consciousness after his fall; the bull is fatally injured; the storm breaks; the boy kills the bull; the boy tells Pete he wants to try to contact the family of the boy on the bridge.*

The single word 'roaring' that concluded the previous section now begins this one, creating a link through repetition, while also shifting the mood. The word in the previous section was alone on a page of vivid, epic, dark imagery, while here it is a single black word on a white page. The next five pages of narrative, similarly, are plain text on white – no illustrations. This indicates a shift from the intense abstract symbolism and emotion of the recent pages into a sharper and more concrete descriptive mode. There is no mistaking or interpreting what is about to happen: it is literal and unambiguous. The language is visceral and traumatic, and it prepares us for the boy's imminent murder of the beast. Both the bull's blood and the drenching rain symbolise a kind of catharsis or cleansing for the boy, making his literal and mental pain 'tolerable' (p.77).

Pete is the one to find the boy, and in the aftermath of the bull's death, the boy somehow feels emboldened to ask the ringer of 'mixed island and indigenous ancestry' (p.25) for advice about trying to track down the family of the boy on the bridge (p.78). Pete, who the boy has previously described as 'seem[ing] indifferent to me' (p.25), is now unexpectedly sympathetic, recognising that the boy has 'been hurtin'. You got somethin' big locked up inside you there' (p.79).

Q Do you read the murder of the bull primarily as a mercy killing of a fellow creature, or as the boy's final triumph over his demons? Explain your choice.

Q What is the significance of the final paragraph of the chapter (p.81), and why do you think it is repeated here (from p.45)?

Key vocabulary

Pie Jesu: a Latin phrase meaning pious (saintly) Jesus.

Pith: kill by severing the spinal cord.

Part Five: Requiem (pp.83–9; also the CD)

Summary: *The CD contains Ottley's musical Requiem, comprising four movements performed by a string ensemble and two vocal soloists; the book contains the lyrics and translations for each of the songs.*

In the same way that the Indigenous man performs songs at the end of the Elder's talk in the community hall, music now follows the narrative of the text. Part Five comprises the music itself, as well as the printed text (pp.83–9). The languages in these pages are Latin, Bundjalung and English, and join with the musical language of the CD. In its incorporation of these three languages, Part Five draws on the narrative threads of the rest of the book, with the Latin representing the classical and mythological elements of the book, the English the boy's everyday experiences, and the Bundjalung the First Nations stories of dispossession and grief. The lyrics themselves are short and quite literal, unlike the more abstract images, structure and events of other parts of the text. Musically, there is a wide range of styles, from Western operatic to traditional Indigenous song; from chaotic and atmospheric sound-pictures to cinematic harmony.

The musical styles overlap, building a similar texture to the book (where multiple voices/modes share the pages), creating sometimes complementary and sometimes discontinuous ideas. For example, at around 2 minutes 52 seconds in the Dies Irae, the Latin and Bundjalung songs are performed simultaneously, accompanied by percussive clapsticks and slightly discordant string phrases, sounding like two completely separate pieces of music, in different keys, languages and rhythms; the lyrics too are telling two different stories ('Ghost Story' and 'Dies Irae'). Although they are linked in tone, they are not direct translations of each other. This recalls pages 65–9, during which the stories of the bridge and of the boy's capture of the bull are told side by side, connecting themes and events purely through literal proximity.

The paired Bundjalung and Latin songs all share the themes of death and the afterlife; of religion, spirituality and faith; and of suffering and loss. These resonate with the ideas in the written and visual sections of the text, although they are not direct retellings. For example, the written text and images do not explore religion, although at times the boy's relationship with the Minotaur (and thus the bull) echoes a spiritual connection, and his quest for the beast – even though he is not quite sure what he is chasing or following or why – echoes a search for faith.

Each of the songs from the chamber piece shares the name of one of the first four sections of the book, making them seem as though they are designed to directly accompany the text. However, the music is designated as Part Five of the book, so it should not simply be read as a soundtrack, even though it is useful to think about how each song relates to its corresponding section. The text's Pie Jesu and the musical composition, for example, are both short and cohesive, and more straightforward stylistically than some others. The Pie Jesu in the text is told primarily in a single modal voice, as a simple third-person narrative. Similarly, the musical Pie Jesu is more conventionally melodic than the other three movements, and the lyrics are the shortest of the songs. Yet text and music contrast with each other in terms of style and tone. The textual Pie Jesu contains the climactic section of the book, with some of the most confronting imagery of the narrative, as the boy kills the injured beast and the storm finally breaks. The musical piece, however, is gentle and soft, beginning with light pizzicato (plucking) strings, and moving to melodic phrases, especially in the higher notes of the strings. The vocal solo is slow, simple and calm. Much of the movement is in a major key, which gives a naturally bright sound to the piece, and there is little to connote the trauma, drama and death of the written chapter.

Although you may not be expected to analyse the music in detail, you can find intersections of tone, mood and structure, and discuss how these contribute to your understanding of the text.

Q Why do you think Ottley labels the musical element of the text as a 'Part' (like the other text sections) rather than including it as a soundtrack to the book?

CHARACTERS & RELATIONSHIPS

The boy

Key quotes

'The boy is afraid ... But he will ride his trepidation to wherever it takes him, because more than anything, he wants to be called "ringer". He is tired of being "the boy", "jackeroo".' (p.18)

'How do I fit in this place ...?' (p.25)

'As a kid I dreamed of being a stockman.' (p.25)

'He stares at the vague form of the man's body, realising that he no longer cares what anyone thinks of him.' (p.78)

The unnamed protagonist is probably in his early twenties, though the text includes several flashbacks to him at earlier stages in his life. Note that, for most of the book, the boy is a young man rather than a child, but he is still described as 'the boy'. This emphasises his sense of a need to grow up and either leave behind or confront his childhood preoccupations (the Minotaur in particular), his troubled relationship with his father, his perceived failures (cheating on his final school results) and his own depression.

He has left home to live and work on a remote cattle station and at first appears both eager and intimidated: this is his 'first season on a big station' (p.18) and 'first experience of wild cattle' (p.23), and while this is a little overwhelming, he can't wait to be taken more seriously as a stationman and not be thought of as young and inexperienced any longer. As soon as he hears about the wild bull that has evaded previous musters, he seems to harbour a peculiar obsession with it – not necessarily with the motivation of killing it, but rather catching up with it. This might be seen as reflecting his desire to face up to his own past.

As a younger child, the boy was somewhat isolated and unsure of himself: as far as we know, he has no siblings, and the only attempted friendship portrayed is one with a new boy at school who dismisses him as worthless (p.58). Within his family, the boy has a positive relationship with his mother, who is supportive of him, whether by sending him books while he is working at the station or by comforting and protecting him as a child from the disappointments of his school life (as illustrated when she holds his shoulders protectively and embraces him, p.58). With his father, however, the relationship is more complex. The boy articulates this himself, when reflecting on the museum visit:

> I was in awe of him, and perhaps for the first time ever actually told myself that I wanted to be him. But at the same time I felt he'd let me down. (p.58)

The boy's father continues to be a shadowy figure in his life, and later, as he grows up, the boy observes that his mother always acted as some sort of intermediary, 'the quiet bridge between him and his father' (p.20), suggesting that there was conflict between them (probably psychological, as there is no suggestion of violence). There is a glimpse of this tension when the father declares that his son 'will not follow in [his] footsteps' as a ringer, even though the boy has seen 'the light that shone from his father's eyes whenever he spoke of the bush and the stock camps' (p.20), and wants to chase that dream too.

The boy apparently suffers from depression and attempted to kill himself before going to work on the station. The suicide attempt is not discussed explicitly (he describes his parents finding him 'almost gone', p.21), and the illustration, too, is somewhat vague: part of his body is shown against a shadowy background as he lies under a messy bedsheet with a glass of water and a packet of unidentified tablets beside him. He hints that his mental health is closely linked with his preoccupation with the Minotaur from his childhood museum visit; his description of 'that strange beast' (p.63) could just as easily apply to a symbolic characterisation of depression as to his persistent memory of the literal Minotaur. Indeed, he observes that the beast 'almost took me' – a thinly veiled allusion to his attempted suicide (p.63).

The boy's parents

Key quotes

'Mum ... feels guilty about the last two years, about what happened to me.' (p.17)

'His mother, always the quiet bridge between him and his father ...' (p. 20)

'And yet the boy remembers the light that shone from his father's eyes whenever he spoke of the bush and the stock camps.' (p.20)

'I was sort of ... removed ... in adoration of a man I couldn't quite trust.' (p.58)

The boy's father carries his own grief and guilt about his association years ago with the murder of an Aboriginal child. In turn his relationship with the boy is complex; he is proud of his son's achievements at school (not knowing the results were faked) but also conflicted about his son following in his footsteps as a stationman. This seems to be because he is conflicted about his past as a ringer: while the boy sees 'how alive he would become whenever he told his stories', the father later becomes 'cynical' about them, 'as if he felt that that part of his life had been a failure' (p.20). He wants his own son to 'make something' of himself, believing that his intellectual strengths should lead him to a more secure and stable vocation. It is likely that the incident with the boy on the bridge is responsible for a large part of the father's increasing regret about his life on stations, and he seems to struggle with internal conflict about his own worth throughout his working life; he is now a 'jack-of-all-trades' (p.25), suggesting that he has never found anything he can fully commit to.

Key point

The connection between the father's grief over his son's struggles and his own haunted memories of the boy on the bridge are illustrated most powerfully and explicitly on page 21, where these ideas converge as the visual images of one blend into those of the other.

The boy's mother does not seem to be a particularly significant part of his life, although what interaction he does have with her is positive. The first thing we hear of her is that she sends the boy books to read (she herself is 'an author', p.25) while he is on the station, apparently out of some form of regret for what the boy has gone through in his recent years – while this is never made explicit, it seems that she is acknowledging his struggles with depression: 'She feels guilty about the last two years, about what happened to me' (p.17). She seems to have a compassionate awareness of the boy's reality that his father never achieves. In fact, when the boy was younger, she was 'always the quiet bridge between him and his father' (p.20), and in what looks set to be a disagreement about their son's future, she tries to 'distract her husband with his food' to de-escalate any conflict (p.20). When he was younger, the boy turned to his mother for comfort after the incident with the toy airplane at the birthday party, and she is shown hugging him protectively (p.58).

It is the boy's mother who must field the father's story about the bridge, when it finally comes bursting out of him, and in the first panel of this story (p.65), she hushes her son and gestures that he shouldn't come any closer to his father, who is facing away. Perhaps she is protecting her son from being exposed to his father's grief, or perhaps she is protecting her husband and giving him some private space; given the boy's characterisation of her as a 'bridge', it seems likely that she is doing both.

There is little information about the relationship between the boy's parents, except as far as it concerns the boy (i.e. the mother trying to maintain peace and a bond between the boy and his father). When the father tells the story about the bridge, it is entirely in monologue. We don't even know how the mother might be responding, as she is not visible in those panels; rather, the father is shown alone with the darkness of his grief while speaking to her. There is a small hint, though, in his language, towards at least some closeness in their relationship, as he regularly calls her 'love' throughout this section, suggesting at least a habitual affection between them.

The old woman / Aboriginal Elder

Key quotes

'I'm supposed to be a fully initiated woman, but that knowledge, that memory, is gone.' (p.42)

'My sister, like my brother and me, was stolen.' (p.43)

'We were completely powerless you see, we'd been taught that we had no rights.' (p.44)

'But it's now time for me and my people to talk, to talk to you, to talk to the land ... to make sure the country is OK. We need to heal ourselves. We will heal you too.' (p.45)

The unnamed Aboriginal Elder is a woman who happens to be speaking at a community hall that the boy passes on his way to the station. Her story is of having been 'stolen' as a child, and reflects the experiences of other children of the Stolen Generations who were taken from families and communities at a young age and raised in homes. Her role in the text is not so much as an individual but as a representative of a time, a place, a particular shameful part of the community's history – a shame the boy first comes to know through her.

Although the story she tells is horrific, and includes violence and trauma, she is portrayed as being very calm and open, and as wanting mainly to educate her non-Indigenous audience (rather than fighting for retribution or trying to incite hatred). She seeks not only to 'heal ourselves' but also to 'heal you too' (p.45). She even acknowledges that 'there are some good stories too from those days' (p.44), and she also wants those to be known. This portrayal makes her seem slightly romanticised and passive, constructed in stark contrast to those in the text who are vilified for their attitudes towards First Nations people (in the case of the father's old ringer mate) or actions against them (in the case of Mick). Similarly, her quiet gentleness contrasts with the masked man / Minotaur coming for the Indigenous boy in the first dream, or the masked man carrying the bloodied axe at the end of Part Three.

The woman wears red, in a rare use of the colour in the text. This could be interpreted as representing the repressed anger and justifiable hatred her family and community might feel against non-Indigenous people. It is a pale and muted red, however, which might instead be read as symbolising her somewhat rose-coloured view of a united future and even of the more positive moments of the past she includes in her story (such as the teacher who helped the schoolchildren escape capture). Perhaps she hopes to make her audience feel less uncomfortable. In constructing her this way, Ottley seeks to elicit empathy from his audience, inclining them to agree with his perspective on the unacceptability of non-Indigenous Australians' treatment of First Nations communities and individuals. This is a perspective that the boy adopts too, cautiously and uncertainly at first when he overhears the story of the bridge, and later with more commitment when he decides he wants to find the boy's family and make a gesture of, if not apology, then at least recognition, which represents a first step towards reconciliation.

The bull

Key quotes

'There is something about its muscular indifference to the world, about its complete dominance of the landscape ... that [the boy] cannot resist.' (p.9)

'"Go with the bull," it says. "You must take the bull."' (p.32)

'The boy sees that all these movements are slow, considered, powerful.' (p.48)

'Occasionally the bull turns its head to look back, as if challenging the boy to keep following.' (p.50)

'That bull' (p.9) is a real bull, but is very closely tied to the mythical Minotaur of the boy's past. Interestingly, the bull is not primarily portrayed as being especially dangerous or violent. Ottley elicits great sympathy for it when it dies.

The bull holds a sort of fabled status with the stockmen: at the previous year's muster he 'nearly killed a man', and since then has only been glimpsed (p.18). The head stockman, Johnno, has declared that if anyone sees the bull this year, they should leave it to him to shoot. It's unclear whether this is because he considers the bull too dangerous or whether it is purely vindictiveness. Either way, Ottley nods to the classic literary narrative *Moby-Dick*, in which the sailor Ahab is driven by an obsessive need to hunt down and kill the whale (Moby Dick) who once took part of his leg. The stories diverge significantly – particularly in the ultimate outcome, as Ahab never succeeds in avenging himself – but share a sense of awe at the strength and power of a large creature, and the experience of being driven by an intention to conquer it.

The bull is a large, wild Brahmin bull, described as being black with 'golden-red' flanks (p.18). That he is shown as being a dark colour suggests that he is an older bull (Brahmins tend to darken as they age). The darkness, of course, is also fittingly symbolic for the psychological darkness he represents for the boy. We first meet him in words – as a huge creature that 'lumbers regally through a sun-enfolded landscape' (p.9). The first visual glimpse of him is not until page 34, when he appears similarly unthreatening, viewed from a strange perspective that makes him seem tiny in comparison to the boy on his grey mare.

The boy sees himself from the beginning as somehow destined to conquer the bull, and this too has double significance: as a young man he is desperate to prove his worth, but in his own emotional torment, tackling the manifestation of the 'beast' that has been with him so long is akin to overcoming his trauma and mental illness. Interestingly, the bull is not conveyed simply as a target. Often the boy seems not to be explicitly wanting to kill the beast but rather is mesmerised into trailing it – both psychologically and also physically through the desert. It is as though he is driven to catch the beast but his sense of purpose ends there: had it not been for the beast's terrible injury, he might not have killed it at all. Simply catching it might have been enough, in terms of conquering it and all it represents.

As the Minotaur has, so too the bull seems to haunt the boy in a complex and (even to the boy) confusing way, both of them seeming to 'follow' him as he is 'hunted ... tracked', yet also leading him forward: they 'drew my spirit' (p.63). Similarly, although the Minotaur has 'pursued' him for years, haunting him – as we see visually on pages 62 and 63 – 'it seemed like something else', something that was 'beautiful, powerful, desirable but unreachable' (p.63). These descriptions of the Minotaur (and the boy's demons) could equally describe the bull. In turn, 'desirable but unreachable' also echoes the boy's conflicted feelings about his father.

The Minotaur

Key quotes

'The Minotaur, a beast that was part human and part bull.' (p.61)

'Why did that strange beast follow me – out of the museum and into the rest of my life? It hunted me, tracked me ... slowly drew my spirit – who I was – from me until there was nothing left.' (p.63)

'But often through the years, as the beast pursued me, it seemed like something else; something that chased me to the edge of fear, but was beautiful, powerful, desirable but unreachable.' (p.63)

The boy first encounters the Minotaur at a museum where his father reads him the story of the Greek mythological creature, and the boy is preternaturally enthralled. The museum visit and the discovery of the myth are linked with a day of rejection and disappointment for the boy, when he feels that his father has let him down, which leads, in turn, to the boy's rejection by a fellow schoolchild. In this way the Minotaur becomes linked with disappointment, sadness and confusion. The museum visit also happens just after a visit to the boy's house by an old ringer mate of his father's, when the boy overhears the man's racist comments about 'blackfellas' (p.57). Although the boy claims, 'I don't remember it having any great effect on me' (p.57), and later (though earlier in the book) that he has 'never really given much thought to indigenous people' (p.17), this moment, on the contrary, seems to have embedded itself in his psyche and offered a disturbing glimpse of a world beyond his own – a world he will later come to know more of than he'd like.

The Minotaur in this story is a 'beast' that haunts the boy – a symbol of the difficult things he has to deal with in his early life, and that he then carries as a young adult because they are not necessarily resolved. Key experiences and emotions the Minotaur represents include:

- the boy's ambivalence about his father as a role model
- the boy's depression
- the boy's feelings of rejection and inadequacy
- the boy's quest for something meaningful in his life that demonstrates his maturity and masculinity.

Key point

Although the Minotaur is a different figure from the bull, they are closely tied in the boy's mind, as is illustrated in their visual similarity. Occasionally, such as on pages 15 or 62, we can only see a beast's head and not a body, so that the image is almost ambiguous, suggesting that at times the boy thinks of the bull and the Minotaur (and his inner demons) as one and the same. In turn, this echoes the moment when he finally faces the bull and feels that he, the horse and the bull are 'all the one creature' (p.32).

The Minotaur appears at many significant moments in the narrative, such as when it smashes through the schoolhouse wall in the boy's initial dream (p.14) and when it looms in the full-page illustration where the boy is tormented by his secret of cheating (p.62) as well as above the car on page 63. Its shadow also dwarfs the image of the father holding his son's hand at the museum (p.60). There are two close-up panels showing these clasped hands (p.22 and p.69); in both, the eye of the Minotaur on the wall of the museum is visible, enduringly inhabiting the boy's memories. The Minotaur and the boy's father are connected in the boy's mind, as suggested by the visual proximity of the two and the fact that this image appears three times in the book.

Other characters

Key quotes

'The boy has noticed how the men have begun talking around the fire at night, about the fights they'll have, the women they'll bed, the "cutting loose" in town when the muster is over.' (p.17)

'... his music seemed to fill the room. It was menacing, and haunting, and incredibly sad at the same time.' (p.21)

'I just kept telling myself that the kid was all right ...' (p.68)

The boy on the bridge

Although he is a key figure in the boy's father's life, and thus in the boy's understanding of his father, the boy on the bridge is almost completely unknown to us (just as he is to the protagonist). He is young – the father estimates between ten and fourteen, though the news report later says the missing boy is sixteen – and is thrown to his almost certain death by one of the ringers, ostensibly because he was 'shyacking around' (mucking around) in a dangerous way on the road, but clearly actually because of the colour of his skin (p.66). The anonymous boy serves as a symbol of the many Indigenous children whose ties to their families and communities were severed by the white policies of forced removal. The boy on the bridge's death haunts both the protagonist and his father, although the father never knows that his son overheard his story.

The stationmen

The stationmen are only vaguely differentiated, and serve largely to represent the culture of the world the boy followed his father into: a tough, sometimes violent, often intolerant community of men who work long, hard seasons of skilled physical labour. Although some of the men in **Johnno**'s crew are Indigenous, there is little discussion of this, other than when the boy chooses to confide in the Indigenous/Islander **Pete** about his curiosity regarding the Indigenous stories he has come across (pp.78–9); Pete responds to this with perhaps unexpected empathy for the boy, recognising that the boy is fighting his own inner demons. The ringers the boy's father worked with are portrayed as having been more menacing and dangerous, particularly in the story about the boy on the bridge, in which head stockman **Mick** – a 'hard man' (p.67) – wilfully and coldly beats the Indigenous boy, verbally abuses him and throws him into the river where he almost certainly drowned.

The Indigenous singer

The boy mentions an old Indigenous man who sang after the Aboriginal Elder's talk in the community hall, and who 'sang in his own language' but also translated the stories into English (p.17). This character correlates with the man in the chamber music composition who sings the Indigenous songs (sometimes first explaining their meaning in English). We know little about him; he merely adds emotional weight to the woman's story, and the boy is haunted by his songs, including one in particular that was 'so full of loneliness' (p.17).

THEMES, IDEAS & VALUES

Trauma

Key quotes

'They showed us where we could go to cry, where no one would see us ...' (p.43)

'I just can't keep it inside me anymore.' (p.65)

'Somehow I managed over the years to forget about it.' (p.68)

'I can see that you been hurtin'. You got somethin' big locked up inside you there.' (p.79)

Trauma dominates in *Requiem for a Beast*, whether for the protagonist or the secondary characters. It is shown to have intense repercussions on individuals' lives, particularly when they have not internally processed their devastating experiences. At times the distress manifests in visual symbols, as with the Minotaur for the boy. At other times it is very literal and is described verbally, such as in the father's story of the boy on the bridge (pp.65–9). At yet other times, the visual and the verbal converge, such as on page 21, where images of the boy on the bridge and the protagonist overlap, and the text box talks about the boy's experience of the 'incredibly sad' Indigenous song, as well as alluding to his own experience of being 'almost gone' (p.21).

Guilt

The father's central traumatic experience is of being involved in the incident of the boy on the bridge and, although he didn't actively chase or throw the boy, he feels implicated because he did not stop it happening, and does not speak of it until years later. To some extent it seems that he has been able to repress his post-traumatic stress – 'I did manage to ... bury it in me somewhere, so I wouldn't have to think about it anymore' (p.68). However it seems likely (and his son suspects) that the incident contributed significantly to the father's ambivalent feelings about his past as a ringer. In some ways he enjoyed that part of his life very much: a 'light shone from his … eyes whenever he spoke of the bush and the stock camps' and the boy remembers 'how alive he would become whenever he told his stories' (p.20). He painted a 'romantic image' of it, and yet as time went on, he also began to be 'increasingly cynical', and declared that his son should never follow in his footsteps in that 'hopeless' life (p.20). It seems likely that his memory of the incident and his guilt at having done nothing to stop it has contributed to an ongoing misery that he cannot seem to overcome. His day of trauma has ricocheted many years later into his life and even into his relationship with his son, which is conflicted and upsetting to the boy, who doesn't know how to feel about his father as a role model. The boy reflects on this ambivalence when he tells the story of the museum visit, as well as when he feels 'enshrouded in shame' during his pursuit of the bull because he believes his father would have 'already thrown the bastard and made a story out of it' (p.64). The boy feels his own guilt at not having somehow lived up to his father's impossible expectations, as well as living with the shadow of his father's guilt about the incident on the bridge years earlier.

Colonial dispossession

Part Two of the text is almost entirely composed of the talk by the Elder in the community hall, which concerns memories and stories of the woman's immediate and generational trauma. Her tale takes in her own and her siblings' experiences of forced removal from their families, as well as the experiences of her grandmother's generation, who were taken to missions and prevented from 'practising their ceremonies', eating 'bush foods' and generally having any connection with their own communities and culture (p.42). Despite this destruction of First Nations culture, the woman emphasises the fact that 'memories … stay with you' (p.42). This is presented as both a positive and a negative: memories have allowed the 'spirit' and the people to survive (p.43), passing those memories down to future generations, too, while on the other hand, memories of a traumatic past are devastating and continue to haunt people like the Elder, who are scarred by their histories.

The (probable) murder of the boy on the bridge also symbolises the extreme discrimination towards and violence committed against First Nations Australians over time. Although this is an individual act – committed by a man who is ignorant and reckless at best, and actively racist and violent at worst – it symbolically represents the many acts that destroyed the lives of First Nations individuals and indeed entire generations. In throwing the boy off the bridge – after chasing him through the bush in an echo of the woman's story of officers who tried 'catching them slippery little black kids in the bush' (p.44) – Mick renders visible the widespread attempted erasure of Indigenous peoples and their cultures.

Recovery

While the text is dominated by trauma, grief and distress, there are several cautious gestures towards the possibilities of catharsis, recovery, reconciliation and even hope for the future. One of the main examples of this is the catharsis the boy experiences during the storm and in the kind of ceremonial and mournful bathing in the blood of the slaughtered bull. After these moments, 'a sense of calm settles on him, an emptiness that does not need to be filled', and he can feel the rain 'washing clean his wounds and although his body aches, the pain is tolerable' (p.77). From the long trauma of his depression and of his life being haunted by the Minotaur, through the violent climax of killing the bull, the boy manages to vanquish some of his trauma and begin to heal. Immediately after this experience, he has a new energy and turns it to finding the family of the boy on the bridge. Having healed himself, he now looks to help someone else recover from trauma.

The other significant example of the idea that recovery and healing are possible is the conclusion to the Aboriginal woman's narrative. She tells her audience that, through talking, communicating and sharing stories, Indigenous and non-Indigenous people alike may be able to 'heal' themselves (p.45). Remarkably, given the suffering she has experienced, she manages to find optimism, believing that a future can be better than even the most terrible past. Although she sees 'another darkness coming' (p.45), she also believes that 'the storm is also a nurturing thing' that 'allows ... the people to grow again', and calls on those present to make a commitment towards surviving that storm: 'We all have to stand in the rain, however long it lasts' (p.45).

Key point

The woman does not elucidate her warning that 'there is another darkness coming' (p.45). She describes a literal storm, talking of clouds, rain and wind, but as with so many other parts of this text, she is speaking in an abstract and symbolic way. Ottley leaves this image quite open for the reader to interpret.

Memories and the past

Key quotes

'He knows this place, but can't remember from where.' (p.9)

'I've dreamed about that song ... a soundtrack to those beasts from my own past.' (p.21)

'The terrible thing about some memories, and the good thing too I suppose, is that they stay with you.' (p.42)

'They tried to belt the memory out of her.' (p.43)

'He rides, entranced by the heat and led by the beast into a world of remembering.' (p.56)

The first words in the text, 'It's our memories that make us' (a quote from the Elder's later story, p.42), indicate the importance of ideas of the past and memories in the book. Much like trauma, the past is shown to have powerful repercussions for the future in *Requiem for a Beast*. The central narrative is of the protagonist being haunted by his childhood experience of encountering the Minotaur – a moment that cements in his mind a particular conception of his own mental health and his challenges in facing the world. Indeed the Minotaur itself is a representation of the past, as it is an ancient Greek story. The museum setting, too, emphasises the role of history in our lives: objects there are 'old, and people love them because they are old. They tell us stories about ourselves and we … see them as beautiful because of that' (p.59).

As well as being demonstrated in many narrative events, the idea of the past is reflected in structural decisions. Specifically, the shifting chronology of the boy's story indicates to us that his past is indelibly tied up with both his present and, likely, his future – as hinted at in the fact that he consults Pete regarding how he might go about tracking down the boy on the bridge's family. In this example, told in the present tense, the boy's potential future is heavily shaped by his past – not only his father's past but his own immediate past: the slaughter of the bull. It seems that, with the cathartic conquering of his demons (real and symbolic), he is suddenly able to focus on a new future that holds opportunities that were invisible to him while he was haunted by his demons.

The boy's father, too, is deeply weighted with his own past. On the one hand, he carries the joyous memories of his energetic ringer days, furnishing his own and his son's imagination with the 'romantic' depictions of his days in the bush: these memories make him 'light' up and become 'alive' when he speaks of them (p.20). Yet, at the same time, somehow his memories of that part of his life drag him down, making him feel as though 'that part of his life had been a failure' (p.20). He remembers how hard the work was and what little future it afforded him, and – particularly in contrast to the bright academic world he believes is open to his son – his past brings him a sadness. This is manifest not just in his own feelings but in the adamance with which he insists that his son will not lead that same life.

More damagingly, the father also carries a deep guilt from his past that seems to have been slowly eroding him from the inside: the memory of the night with the boy on the bridge. Here, his past encroaches on his present as he ages, and it surfaces after years of repression. In his desperation, he finally tells the story to the boy's mother, but there is little sense that his confession lightens or heals him: he does not enter the text again. This suggests that it is impossible to erase or cleanse one's past, either through repressing or disclosing memories.

The Elder's story further explores the idea of memory and the past as being indelible. Not only can she, her family and her community never forget or emotionally escape their past – 'The darkness of those years ... followed me' (p.45) – but it tangibly harms many of them: they 'no longer knew their place in the world' (p.43) and as a result often resorted to suicide. The land she was taken away from was not just her home but her 'mother's country, and her mother's too' (p.42) – a whole history. The woman scorns the idea that 'countless generations of knowledge that is in us' can be wiped clean (p.42). For her, personal and generational memory is constitutive – that is, it forms part of a person's identity. Yet she complicates this idea by also suggesting that time in the missions and camps left the children with 'no bonding' capacity with their families because they no longer remembered the reality of that connection (p.43), and also that her own right to be a 'fully initiated woman' has been thwarted because 'that knowledge, that memory, is gone' (p.42). Thus, while the future cannot be separated from the past, parts of the past may still be lost or taken away.

Interconnectedness and transition

Key quotes

'The boy and his horse have become one ...' (p.32)

'They lurch around in circles, writhing, like a single beast.' (p.70)

By its very nature, a multimodal text argues for the existence of a complex and interconnected world. The boy's story is told not just in a straightforward narrative thread but through many voices and in overlapping time frames. Our understanding of both his present and his past can only be reached by the linking of the narrative's disparate parts: text, illustration and music, as well as in the intersection of the past and present, as demonstrated by the nonlinear chronology.

Often in *Requiem for a Beast*, the overlaps between ideas, events, characters, landscapes and histories can be confusing, and it is not always possible to tease them apart into their separate components and meanings. For example, the mythical Minotaur who inhabits the boy's mind is a central figure, but without the real bull – particularly the scene in which the boy slays it – it would be difficult to make sense of the boy's preoccupation with the Minotaur. As it is, the meanings are still somewhat abstract, but the relation is very clear. The two connect reality and imagination, they represent shared concepts (fear and conquering fear), and they integrate to symbolise the boy's psychological struggles.

Often when events, ideas and even characters overlap, it is in a dream of the boy's, such as in the very early pages, where the sound of a car gradually transforms into a horse, then the call of a rider; the rider then transforms from a man to a beast-man to a man-beast to the beast itself. In that same dream, the Indigenous child is anonymous but linked (by his cries for his mother) with the Elder and with the boy on the bridge, all of them having been taken from their families. This connecting of ideas allows for a theme to be strongly emphasised.

The idea of connection between man and beast is elucidated in the myths of the centaurs and the Minotaur, both mythological creatures who are half-human and half-animal, introduced to the boy's world through the museum visit. Such connections are illustrated repeatedly in the text. Examples include:

- the old man's song, describing 'the first time his ancestors saw a white man'; because he was riding a horse, they interpreted him as a 'two headed ghost' (p.21)
- the boy himself, imagining that he has 'become such a beast' (a Minotaur), in a dramatic visual illustration of transition on page 23 →

- the moment when the boy, his mare and the bull face off: 'The boy and his horse have become one, and together, by an invisible cord, have joined with the bull. They are all the one creature ... He cannot feel the difference between his own body and that of the horse' (p.32)
- the wordless zoom panels in which the eye of the bull contains the eye of the Indigenous boy, itself containing a sky (pp.35–7)
- the dream in which Rudy melds with his horse to become a monster of some kind – a messy blend of horse, man and bull (pp.51–3).

Even when creatures are not directly 'merging' as such, distinct connections are implied by the illustrations. For example, on page 15 is a close-up of the Minotaur's head, echoed powerfully on page 28 with the head of a horse, with a similar composition and tone, even though the colours differ. At other times, the Minotaur also merges with the landscape, such as on pages 63 or 72, and there are symbolic moments when humans fuse with environment too, such as when the boy's tears and the rain merge together in the storm, washing over him as he kills the bull (p.77).

One confusing conflation is between the boy on the bridge (only seen in illustration once, on p.21) and the apparently younger Indigenous boy who is first seen on the cover and later in the schoolhouse, then in the eye of the bull, and finally holding the rope tied to the Minotaur (p.72). This is an example of one of the ideas left up to the reader's interpretation and never resolved. Are the two simply representative of the Stolen Generations? Is the younger boy a race-blind representation of the protagonist himself, often appearing helpless and often 'tied' (sometimes literally) with the bull and the Minotaur? This interpretation could be supported by the fact that at key points in the story (the museum visit and when he finally confronts the bull) the protagonist is wearing a green shirt, just as the boy in the schoolhouse is.

Growth

Key quotes

'This is his first season on a big station ... more than anything, he wants to be called "ringer". He is tired of being "the boy", "jackeroo".' (p.18)

'But the storm is also a nurturing thing, a thing that allows the land and the people to grow again.' (p.45, p.81)

Although the action in *Requiem for a Beast* takes place over a relatively short period of time (with occasional flashbacks), it still shows a dramatic development in the boy, as he moves, at least to some extent, beyond the traumas of the past that have plagued him. He matures into someone with new agency in the world, as demonstrated when he takes charge of his father's shameful story, looking for an opportunity to bring something positive to the situation in order to help others to heal. This is closely tied to the Aboriginal Elder, who tells her story as a means to open up a dialogue and begin to acknowledge the wrongs of the past and look to a better future. Having heard her speak of healing, the boy is compelled to find her, in the hope not only of speaking with her about her own story, but of finding the family of the boy on the bridge and telling them the story he knows. (Pete suggests, too, that this may be healing for the protagonist, who Pete senses has his own story he needs to tell.)

The boy would not have been able to put in place this quest had he not first overcome his own demons: the Minotaur of his past that has come to be associated with his depression and that he is able to confront in the form of the bull. In killing the bull he sees himself as a grown man, no longer the 'boy' of the station, but someone who can take down a creature that has thwarted others. This suggests that in order to grow, one must face difficult things.

A second area of growth for the boy is in his dawning understanding of a recent Indigenous history he had known nothing about. Previously, his awareness had been limited to overhearing the old ringer mate of his father's crudely describing 'blackfellas' as 'monkeys', and his father defending this (p.57). Later, he overhears his father telling the story of the boy on the bridge and, while it seems to haunt the boy, he is apparently never quite sure why. Stumbling upon the Elder speaking in the community hall, suddenly the boy's perspective is dramatically widened as he becomes aware of some of the experiences of the Stolen Generations, and he appears to connect this to the night on the bridge, as he later approaches Pete for advice about trying to contact both the Elder and the family of the boy. He has taken steps towards greater understanding, and actively wants to widen and deepen his knowledge. This exchange with Pete takes place in the final pages of the story, followed by a quote from the Elder's talk: 'the storm is also a nurturing thing, a thing that allows the land and the people to grow again' (p.81). The boy has endured his own symbolic storms (and the recent literal one) and is ready to continue growing.

Stories

Key quotes

'He wants his own stories.' (p.20)

'That story, which I'm not supposed to know, and the old woman's tale ... have changed everything for me ...' (p.21).

'But there are some good stories too from those days, you know, and they need to be told as well.' (p.44)

'We've all got our stories, eh?' (p.79)

Stories are what drive characters forward in this text; they are what help them understand the world, each other and themselves.

Although they intersect, many of the elements of the text can be seen as distinct stories, some of which are outlined in greater detail on the next two pages.

Theseus and the Minotaur

Although it is primarily the figure of the Minotaur itself, rather than the Greek legend about this creature, that becomes fixed in the boy's mind, the spectre of this story still hangs over the narrative. In the myth, the Minotaur lived in a labyrinth, into which youths were sent to die, as sacrifices. To an extent, the boy ventures into the labyrinth of his own psyche, and throughout the text he attempts to navigate its twists and turns, ultimately tracking down his own personal Minotaur and, like Theseus, destroying the beast.

In another sense, the boy's father loosely reflects an element of the myth: King Minos. It was Minos who, in his desperation to bury a shameful event, had the labyrinth built to hide the beast (the literal offspring of that shame). The boy's father, similarly, builds a symbolic psychological maze within his own mind (represented by his emotional distress) to bury his own secret shame of the night the boy on the bridge was killed.

The boy on the bridge

The story of the boy on the bridge is one belonging to the father, but after overhearing it, his son internalises its impact and some of the shame surrounding it; eventually, after tackling a significant challenge in his own life, the boy sets out to try to right some of the wrong done that night.

The incident is presented as a story: told in first person with no interruptions, as the father directly recounts what happened. Although it is self-contained, it is told in direct parallel with the visual story of his son's battle with the bull at the edge of the escarpment. These two distinct narratives together paint a portrait of struggle: whether with a physical challenge or a mental one.

The Stolen Generations

The Aboriginal Elder whom the boy comes across in the community hall has a story to tell about her own and her family's life, but which is also representative of a much larger story: the history of the Stolen Generations. As she describes to her audience the terrible things she and her siblings went through, she is using storytelling to educate and to motivate. By talking to people who may not know these histories, she gives them insight into the experiences of others and offers an opportunity to consider how to change things going forward. Though the 'darkness' of her history is devastating and pervasive, she believes that by sharing these stories she may begin to heal herself, her direct community and the wider Australian community: 'it's now time for me and my people to talk … to bring our language back into this country' (p.45).

The old man who sings after her talk is telling stories too, about 'kin and connection' (p.21). His songs have a distinct impact on the boy, who later says 'I've dreamed about that song', and its story has infused itself into his own experience: 'ominous but beautiful, a soundtrack to those beasts from my own past' (p.21).

DIFFERENT INTERPRETATIONS

Different interpretations arise from different responses to a text. Over time, a text will evoke a wide range of responses from its readers, who may come from various social or cultural groups and live in very different places and historical periods. Responses by critics and reviewers can be published in newspapers, journals and books, both online and in print. They can also be expressed in discussions among readers in the media, classrooms, book groups and so on.

While there is no single correct reading or interpretation of a text, it is important to understand that an interpretation is more than a personal opinion – it is the justification of a point of view on the text. To present an interpretation of a text based on your point of view, you must use a logical argument and support it with relevant evidence from the text.

The critics' viewpoints

As author and writing teacher Sally Murphy for the independent reviewing site *Aussie Reviews* says, *Requiem for a Beast* 'almost defies description' (Murphy 2007). This comment demonstrates how overwhelming it can be to analyse something so complex and layered in its composition.

Requiem for a Beast is a challenging text, not easily boxed into one genre or another, and as such has generated a range of responses. However, the primary controversy has been over its appropriateness for its potential audience. There was much criticism when the CBCA (Children's Book Council of Australia) gave it the Picture Book of the Year award in 2008, as many thought that the book did not belong in this category. While its physical format is that of a picture book, its content is not regarded as suitable for the young children generally considered to be the market for a traditional 'picture book'.

Defending the text, Head of the Queensland Writers Centre Kate Eltham commented:

> Detractors ask if we really want to read profanity and racist dialogue in our children's books? But this is an insidious question. What can the reasonable answer be except 'no'? ... But this of course masks the real issue. That ugliness exists. That racism, violence and ignorance are real. And books, especially fiction, are still the best vehicles for exploring confronting ideas. (ABC News 2008)

Its thematic and narrative complexity has meant that the book has prompted more academic study and analysis than one might normally expect of a picture book. For example, Elizabeth Hale, in her chapter for the book *Chasing Mythical Beasts: The Reception of Ancient Monsters in Children's and Young Adults' Culture*, noted:

> *Requiem for a Beast* attempts something unusual, but also important, in children's literature: the author uses universal myths to enhance cultural understanding and shows how facing a mythical beast from the classical tradition enables a modern Australian boy to take steps towards overcoming the real beasts of personal and national history. (Hale 2020, p.158)

Hale's discussion of the book, rather than being interested in its age-appropriateness, focuses on the way that it draws from classical mythology as a textual source to underpin the narrative of the boy.

On the other hand, academic study has also responded to the controversy over the book. Erica Hateley from the Queensland University of Technology, for example, discusses both the background and the possible implications of regulating the readership of a book. In a conference presentation and paper, she suggested that the debate over the appropriateness of the book for younger readers was a timely reminder of the need of 'teacher librarians, and caregivers to examine (and, often, defend) their roles and responsibilities in the circulation and promotion of children's literature' (Hateley 2014).

Two interpretations of *Requiem for a Beast*

Interpretation 1: *Requiem for a Beast* shows that the cycle of pain is inescapable.

Pain is a central theme in *Requiem for a Beast*. Whether personal trauma, generational trauma, loss, guilt, mental health or physical violence, barely a page of this dark (literally and symbolically) text is without great distress. The protagonist himself is pursued by a terrifying mythical beast born of a moment in his childhood and fed over the years by his insecurities, fears and depression. The Minotaur haunts his days (as when he tries to divulge to his parents that he cheated in his school results, and the beast is seen, huge and black, glowering down at him) and especially his dreams. These range from visions of Indigenous children being hunted to horses and riders merging into malevolent beasts, and he is always tortured by the shadow of the Minotaur. The symbolic creature seems to manifest itself as a bull that the boy encounters while working on a cattle station, and into which he seems to transfer some of his preoccupation with the Minotaur, setting in motion a quest that the reader knows can only end with the beast's death. In finally killing it, however, the boy is devastated and overcome with sorrow for the beast; thus his brief reprieve from traumatic pursuit by the Minotaur is immediately replaced by grief for the bull and a sense of shame and responsibility for the wrong he has committed against it ('I'm so sorry I have to do this to you', p.76). No matter how hard the boy has fought to overcome his inner demons, they will always be replaced by some new pain. Even in his commitment to finding the family of the boy on the bridge, he is fully aware that, although it is something he must do, he may be getting his own father into 'serious trouble' (p.78). The cycle of pain goes on, as one wound always breeds another.

Interpretation 2: *Requiem for a Beast* offers a hopeful world where redemption from past horror is possible.

The boy in this story has suffered, for many years, from a strange obsession with a hideous Minotaur, which may represent his struggles with his mental health, but also echoes his guilt about cheating at school, insecurity about his future and his identity, and a conflicted relationship with his father, who he idolises but does not fully trust. It is clear that until he can overcome this frightening creature – whatever it may represent – he will not be able to move on with his life. Fortunately, while working on a cattle station, he encounters a bull into whom he seems able to channel his fears, ambitions and resistance to a world that tries to crush him. In pursuing (and sometimes being hypnotically and even peacefully drawn along by) this physical manifestation of the beast that haunts his inner world, the boy is able finally to conquer the monsters in his mind. Whether or not he fully intended all along to kill the beast, he finally does so, and is rewarded with the intense catharsis of the storm breaking and symbolically washing him clean. He has exorcised his demons and is free to move on and achieve more positive things in the world around him – such as helping the family of the boy on the bridge to heal by bringing them the potential peace of knowing at last what happened to their son.

QUESTIONS & ANSWERS

This section focuses on your own analytical writing on the text, and gives you strategies for producing high quality responses in your coursework and exam essays.

Essay writing – an overview

An essay on a literary work is a formal and serious piece of writing that presents your point of view on the text, usually in response to a given topic. Your 'point of view' in an essay is your interpretation of the meaning of the text's language, structure, characters, situations and events, supported by detailed analysis of textual evidence.

Analyse – don't summarise

In your essays it is important to avoid simply summarising what happens in a text.

- A **summary** is a description or paraphrase (retelling in different words) of the characters and events. For example: 'Macbeth has a horrifying vision of a dagger dripping with blood before he goes to murder King Duncan.'
- An **analysis** is an explanation of the real meaning or significance that lies 'beneath' the text's words (and images, for a film). For example: 'Macbeth's vision of a bloody dagger shows how deeply uneasy he is about the violent act he is contemplating, and conveys his sense that supernatural forces are impelling him to act.'

A limited amount of summary is sometimes necessary to let your reader know which part of the text you wish to discuss. However, always keep this to a minimum and follow it immediately with your analysis of what this part of the text is really telling us.

Plan your essay

Carefully plan your essay so that you have a clear idea of what you are going to say. The plan ensures that your ideas flow logically, that your argument remains consistent and that you stay on the topic. An essay plan should be a list of **brief dot points** covering no more than half a page.

- Include your central argument or main contention – a concise statement of your overall response to the topic.
- Write three or four dot points for each paragraph, indicating the main idea and evidence/examples from the text. Note that in your essay you will need to *expand* on these points and *analyse* the evidence.

Structure your essay

An essay is a complete, self-contained piece of writing. It has a clear beginning (the introduction), middle (several body paragraphs) and end (the last paragraph or conclusion). It must also have a central argument that runs throughout, linking each paragraph to form a coherent whole. See examples of introductions and conclusions in the 'Analysing a sample topic' and 'Sample answer' sections.

The introduction establishes your overall response to the topic. It includes your main contention and outlines the main evidence you will refer to in the course of the essay. Write your introduction *after* you have done a plan and *before* you write the rest of the essay.

The body paragraphs argue your case – they present evidence from the text and explain how this evidence supports your argument. Each body paragraph needs:

- a strong **topic sentence** (usually the first sentence) that states the main point being made in the paragraph
- **evidence** from the text, including some brief quotations
- **analysis** of the textual evidence, with **explanation** of its significance and how it supports your argument
- **links back to the topic** in one or more statements, usually towards the end of the paragraph.

Connect the body paragraphs so that your discussion flows smoothly. Use some linking words and phrases such as 'similarly' and 'on the other hand', though don't start every paragraph like this. Another strategy is to use a significant word from the last sentence of one paragraph in the first sentence of the next.

Use key terms from the topic – or synonyms for them – throughout, so the relevance of your discussion to the topic is always clear.

The conclusion ties everything together and finishes the essay. It includes strong statements that emphasise your central argument and provide a clear response to the topic.

Avoid simply restating the points made earlier in the essay – this will end on a very flat note and imply that you have run out of ideas and vocabulary. The conclusion should be a logical extension of what you have written, not just a repetition or summary of it. Writing an effective conclusion can be a challenge. Try using these tips:

- Start by linking back to the final sentence of the second-last paragraph – this helps your writing to flow, rather than leaping back to your main contention straight away.
- Use synonyms and expressions with equivalent meanings to vary your vocabulary. This allows you to reinforce your line of argument without being repetitive.
- When planning your essay, think of one or two broad statements or observations about the text's wider meaning. These should be related to the topic and your overall argument. Keep them for the conclusion, since they will give you something 'new' to say but still follow logically from your discussion. The introduction will be focused on the topic, but the conclusion can present a wider view of the text.

Essay topics

1 How do the boy's dreams help construct *Requiem for a Beast*?

2 "I've never told you this before. But I … I just can't keep it inside me anymore."
What role do secrets play in the narrative of *Requiem for a Beast*?

3 Discuss the significance of the title of Matt Ottley's book.

4 How does Ottley use colour to help tell the story in *Requiem for a Beast*?

5 'The text is so abstract that it is impossible to ever understand the main character.' Discuss.

6 'The boy never manages to truly recover from his past.'
To what extent do you agree?

7 Discuss the intersection of text and image in this multimodal text.

8 'Symbolism is the most important element in this text.'
To what extent do you agree?

9 "I understand now what my own story – them finding me on my bed, almost gone – must have done to my father …"
How does understanding contribute to relationships in this text?

10 How does *Requiem for a Beast* explore the experience of grief?

Vocabulary for writing on *Requiem for a Beast*

Graphic novel: a text that contains both words and illustrations; usually constructed in panels as in a comic book.

Stolen Generations: First Nations children who were forcibly removed from their families over many decades, under governmental policies aimed at achieving the assimilation of First Nations communities and peoples into the dominant white culture.

Musical terms

Ensemble: a group of musicians playing together; a chamber ensemble is a small ensemble (usually fewer than ten musicians).

Melodic: tuneful.

Movement: a section of a musical work – similar to a chapter in a text; the chamber work with this text has four movements.

Pace: the speed of the music.

Pitch: how high or low sounds are.

Terms relating to the visual elements

Composition: the way an image is put together, such as which elements are central, what perspective is represented, how full or sparse the image is, and what is included.

Layout or placement: the way elements of text are arranged on a page; for example, a layout might focus on a large image with text only in a small font, or it might place all the text in a central area and images to the sides.

Palette: a range of colours chosen by an artist.

Panel: a box containing imagery and/or text.

Text box: a border containing text and separating it from an image.

Typeface: often used interchangeably with ***font***; although, strictly speaking typeface is the broad grouping for a style or design of the letters, while font accounts for the specific features such as size and spacing.

Analysing a sample topic

How do the boy's dreams help construct *Requiem for a Beast*?

This topic is focused on one specific component of the text – dreams – but remember that you need to demonstrate your understanding of the text as a whole (and, with a multimodal text, your answer will need to at least acknowledge the roles of the various modes), so you will need to link your argument with the broader themes of the text. In this case, you might start by brainstorming the idea of dreams in relation to other features of the text: how do the dream sequences relate to settings, structure, characters and relationships, and themes and ideas?

This topic is a fairly open one, with no expectation for you to agree or disagree with, or even discuss, an assertion about the text. Instead, you will need to form your own statement summarising an answer to the question posed – this is your main contention and will be explained in your introduction and then supported by the ideas in your body paragraphs. Your contention is likely to be more complex in response to an open topic, as you will need to be very specific about the way you are approaching it.

Rather than trying to come up with a contention out of nowhere, start by writing down any questions that come to mind when you see the topic – for example, what are the dream sequences; how do we know they are dreams; how do they differ from other parts of the text; what do they convey; what would the text be like without them. Answers to these questions might help you to narrow down your interpretation of the text in response to the topic, and help you make sure it is clear. Here, your contention might argue that dreams serve to show us the boy's true character; that they bring together multiple modes (illustration and text); that they develop thematic tensions; that they mark structural transitions; or that they construct the overall tone.

The sample discussion below is a little broader, addressing the idea that the dreams are symbolic and that this symbolism facilitates diverse readings of the text.

Sample introduction

In the multimodal text *Requiem for a Beast*, parts of the protagonist's story are told through dreams, which are often abstract and always non-naturalistic. The boy's dreams make use of both the visual and the textual modes of the story, with wildly emotive illustrations accompanying his first person narration of what is happening. They offer us a glimpse into the boy's mind, helping us to understand some of the suffering, trauma and fear he experiences. While they may contextualise plot events and allow us to draw connections between multiple themes and ideas in the text, the dream sequences are sometimes convoluted and difficult to interpret, reminding us inherently that a reading of a text is always a subjective interpretation.

Body paragraph outline

Paragraph 1: One of the earliest sections of the text is a dream, indicating the importance of this mode to the narrative.

- The dream is a form of foreshadowing, introducing ideas without yet contextualising them (e.g. the Stolen Generations, the Minotaur, the boy's depression).
- Its abstract tone/structure symbolises the boy's state of mind: his fears, his conflation of ideas (e.g. his school results and the Stolen Generations) and the vividness of his imaginative life.
- It establishes the visual setting of the station, though we are told the boy 'knows this place, but can't remember from where' (p.9): while dreams may represent reality, they are also distorted.
- It emphasises the text's modality, comprising third-person narrative, wordless images, and first-person narrative with illustration. The protagonist also later says 'I've dreamed … a soundtrack to those beasts from my own past' (p.21), alluding to links between dreams and the musical component of the text.

Paragraph 2: Dreams in the text distil key ideas into abstract representation, often open to interpretation, as seen in the second dream.

- Rudy's initial delight at the horse's wildness could represent the boy's father's love of station work and how 'alive he would become' when telling stories of his experiences (p.20); the horse takes over and consumes Rudy, just as the boy's father's past consumes him.
- Rudy's transformation into the Minotaur (p.53) echoes the man's transition in the first nightmare (pp.14–15) and also the boy's own brief transformation as the Minotaur haunts his thoughts (p.23); this shows the constant presence of the beast in the boy's life.
- The Aboriginal woman (p.54) is unfamiliar but (with matching shirt colour and hair length) might be a younger version of the Elder from the community hall; alternatively she could be the mother of the Elder, the mother of the boy in the first dream or the mother of the boy on the bridge.

Paragraph 3: This text is complex and often abstract; the dream sections give readers permission to be confused but also to interpret meaning from the book.

- The woman delivers from the protagonist his 'remorse, bringing it wet and squirming into the daylight', telling him it is his 'child' (p.55).
- The 'child' might represent his depression, which, once brought into the open, seems cavernous and unhealable like 'the wound that was left' when the remorse was removed (p.55).
- 'Remorse', however, also connotes the wrongs committed against this woman; his remorse might be a kind of generational guilt for his father's complicity in the murder of the boy on the bridge, itself a symbol of the colonial dispossession of First Nations peoples.
- Alternatively, he may simply be experiencing empathetically the feelings he imagines accompany the loss of a child.

Sample conclusion

The rich symbolism within the dreams in *Requiem for a Beast* helps to convey the important ideas in the text – from struggles with mental health to the difficult histories of treatment of Indigenous peoples. The dreams draw on multiple modes, particularly the vivid illustrations and the intimate first-person narrative, and help us to understand the characters and events of the text. Yet, at the same time they are abstract and complex, and resist being boxed into singular readings, opening up a world beyond the text where subjective interpretation is the key to digesting the narrative.

SAMPLE ANSWER

"I've never told you this before. But I ... I just can't keep it inside me anymore."
What role do secrets play in the narrative of *Requiem for a Beast*?

The protagonist of *Requiem for a Beast* is surrounded by secrets: both others' and his own. As the ringer Pete observes, the boy has 'somethin' big locked up inside'. The text is filled with suffering both directly and tangentially related to hidden truths, suggesting that it is never healthy to keep secrets, particularly traumatic ones, and that such suppression can create inner demons that are virtually inescapable. Often these demons are portrayed in the threatening, dark, intense colour palettes of the illustrations, as well as in verbal narrative. The text is reluctant to suggest that silences can be broken and equilibrium can be restored: on the contrary, their dangerous power may be transferred to others and perpetuated.

From early in the book, the boy feels he must hide parts of himself; he resists a temptation to confide in the head stockman's wife, Ellie: 'I must keep my story to myself.' Clearly he respects the privacy of the men he works with in this harsh land, isolating himself in the process. But his 'story' is much deeper, encompassing his curious preoccupation with a mythical beast; his depression and attempted suicide; and his having forged his school results. The Minotaur that looms over the boy in his waking and sleeping hours represents the crushing pressure of the secrets he keeps. He desperately wishes he could tell his parents – 'if only you both knew' – about his results, but is trapped in his own lies, and the beast glares menacingly at him as he types, almost daring him to confess. Hiding the truth from his family and those around him wreaks havoc with the boy's already vulnerable mental health.

The secret the boy inherits from his father – of the harassment and (likely) murder of an Indigenous boy in the past – also haunts him mercilessly, since the boy never admits to overhearing the story. Illustrations throughout link the boy's own inner torments with this one, clearly showing the far-reaching damage such secrets cause. For example, in a dark, busy page, the images of the protagonist after (presumably) overdosing and of the boy on the bridge blur together, showing that keeping fear and pain to oneself can lead as far as self-harm – this is supported later with the tale of the Elder's sister. The boy suspects that his own suicide attempt 'hooked into that episode' from his father's past, compounding his grief.

The father has never forgiven himself for not intervening on the bridge; he unsuccessfully 'tried to put it out of [his] mind' immediately afterwards, though did later manage to 'bury it in [him] somewhere, so [he] wouldn't have to think about it anymore'. However, it has obviously been corrupting him emotionally. He increasingly becomes bitter about his days as a ringer, and the joyous stories he told his young son about those times become unsustainable lies, as the incident taints all the father's memories, and the boy imagines he feels 'that that part of his life had been a failure'. Finally, in his desperation for some kind of release of the terrible memories inside him, the father confesses to his wife, not realising that his son overhears. The overlapping panel borders and the simultaneous stories of the bridge and of the boy's battle to tie up the bull in Part Three show how intricately the dark secret has woven together the man and his son; they also both wear green tops in these pages, insisting we connect them.

This story, lodged in the son's consciousness and his nightmares, connects with that of the Aboriginal Elder in the community hall. As a child, the woman's sister was beaten by the authorities to stop her telling others about the 'outside world'. Being forced to conceal her experience contributed to her suicide, and 'hers was a common story' – many other 'stolen people' were likely destroyed by living in silence about the horrors committed against them. In bringing these stories to light and talking openly about the past, the woman hopes to purge some of her community's suffering so they may begin 'to heal'. For her, the idea of supressing the past is directly aligned with continuing to feel the pain of it. Her attempts to cleanse herself of these memories are echoed in the fact that her narrative is told almost entirely in text on clean white pages, rather than being accompanied by the dark, dominant images of other sections of the text.

Other than the woman's attempts, the text rarely shows the possibility of escaping secrets and their insidious power. The boy never tells his parents about his school results, so we don't know if his confession would be met with forgiveness; similarly, although the father finally reveals his secret, he is then absent from the text, preventing any evidence of catharsis. However, there is a small glimmer of hope when, having conquered the bull (and thus symbolically some of his past trouble), the boy believes he may be able to talk with the family of the boy on the bridge, in an attempt to mutually repair the damage that generational guilt and secrets have wrought. Overwhelmingly, though, *Requiem for a Beast* suggests that withholding truths is always detrimental.

REFERENCES & READING

Text

Ottley, M 2007, *Requiem for a Beast*, Lothian Children's Books, Sydney.

References

ABC News 2008, 'Award-winning picture book's "ugly themes" defended', *ABC News Online*, 27 August, https://www.abc.net.au/news/2008-08-27/award-winning-picture-books-ugly-themes-defended/490286

Hale, E 2020, 'Facing the Minotaur in the Australian Labyrinth: Politics and the Personal in Requiem for a Beast', in Marciniak, K (ed.), *Chasing Mythical Beasts: The Reception of Ancient Monsters in Children's and Young Adults' Culture*, pp.157–73.

Hateley, E 2014, '*Requiem for a Beast*: A case study in controversy', in Suzuki, A (ed.), *The Asian Conference on Literature and Librarianship 2014: Official Conference Proceedings*, pp.1–13.

Lawn, J 2022, 'Matt Ottley and his books', *Paperbark*, 21 February, https://paperbarkwords.blog/2022/02/21/matt-ottley-and-his-books%EF%BF%BC/

Murphy, S 2007, 'Review: Requiem for a Beast, by Matt Ottley', *Aussie Reviews*, https://aussiereviews.com/2007/10/requiem-for-a-beast-by-matt-ottley/

Ottley, M, official website, https://mattottley.com/home/

Rudd, K 2008, 'Apology to Australia's Indigenous Peoples', Parliament of Australia, https://www.aph.gov.au/Visit_Parliament/Art/Exhibitions/Custom_Media/Apology_to_Australias_Indigenous_Peoples

Other resources

Adams, P 2008, *'Requiem for a Beast'*, *Late Night Live* (ABC RN), 5 November, https://www.abc.net.au/radionational/programs/latenightlive/requiem-for-a-beast/3172898

'Bringing Them Home', https://bth.humanrights.gov.au/

Derouet, L & McCallum, J (eds.) 2008, 'Judges' report', Children's Book Council of Australia, https://cbca.blob.core.windows.net/media/Default/Documents/Book%20of%20the%20Year/2008/CBCA_JudgesReport_only_2008.pdf

Whitehead, K 2021, 'Australian artist Matt Ottley on battling bipolar disorder, fighting bulls in the Outback and finally finding happiness', *Post Magazine*, 30 October, https://www.scmp.com/magazines/post-magazine/arts-music/article/3154173/australian-artist-matt-ottley-battling-bipolar